Neighborhood Initiative
and the
Love of God

Neighborhood
Initiative
and the
Love of God

LYNN CORY
A Challenge from Dallas Willard

ISBN-13: 978-1-61291-644-6

Cover design by Nadine Erickson

Some of the anecdotal illustrations in this book are true to life and are included with the permission of the persons involved. All other illustrations are composites of real situations, and any resemblance to people living or dead is coincidental.

Unless otherwise identified, all Scripture quotations in this publication are taken from the *Holy Bible, New International Version*® (NIV®). Copyright © 1973, 1978, 1984, 2011 by Biblica, Inc.® Used by permission of Zondervan. All rights reserved worldwide. www.zondervan.com. The "NIV" and "New International Version" are trademarks registered in the United States Patent and Trademark Office by Biblica, Inc.® Other versions used include: *THE MESSAGE* (MSG), copyright © 1993, 1994, 1995, 1996, 2000, 2001, 2002, used by permission of NavPress Publishing Group; the New American Standard Bible® (NASB), copyright © 1960, 1962, 1963, 1968, 1971, 1972, 1973, 1975, 1977, 1995 by The Lockman Foundation, used by permission; 21st Century King James Version (KJ21). Copyright © 1994 by Deuel Enterprises, Inc.; and the King James Version (KJV).

Printed in the United States of America

3 4 5 6 7 8 / 18 17 16 15

Neighborhood Initiative is dedicated to my Talbot Seminary professor Dr. Joe Aldrich, who modeled how to love our actual neighbors as ourselves. Dr. Aldrich broke down walls between pastors in cities across America, leading them to pray for one another, the church in their cities, and those desperately in need of a Shepherd.

Contents

A Challenge from Dallas Willard

I am so thankful to have this opportunity to share my thoughts with you about the important work Lynn Cory has been doing over the past several years. My heart is with the Neighborhood Initiative under Christ. It's the only thing that can bring life to our cities now. Neighborhood Initiative has been raised up in our time by the Spirit of God to address the special conditions of our cities. One way of putting that is to say that our cities have, in a manner of speaking, outgrown neighbors. It's hard now today to know who our neighbors are and how we're to approach them and be with them. The key to understanding the teachings of Jesus still remains: Loving our neighbor as ourselves in the power of God. And when you think about what that means, you realize that if that were done, almost every problem that we have in our cities would be solved. All we have to do is to simply follow Jesus' words.

Of course, loving God with all our heart, soul, mind, and strength comes first. Without that, you can't love your neighbor as yourself. You have to have the resources, the insight to do that, and that comes from our love of God and our devotion of every aspect of our being to His work which He's doing in our world. God is present in our cities. He is there as the great God who created the world and our cities and everything in them. And now He's inducting us and bringing us into His work as we learn in His presence to love our neighbor as ourself. When He says the Great Commandment is to love God with all your heart, soul, mind, and strength and your neighbor as yourself, that's one of His great statements about how this is *all* you have to do. If you just do this, everything else will take care of itself. One of the things that we often miss is that His mission in the world is incarnational. It comes through people. Incarnation is not just a theological doctrine. It's a doctrine about how we live. And if we're going to bring Christ to our world, our cities and our neighbors, then we do it in our own person: skin on skin contact, face to face relationships with others in which we manifest a love that is beyond human possibility and yet is within human actuality because God makes it so.

So the local congregation is the source of God's incarnational presence in our world. We're apt to miss that and I'm afraid too often in our programs of reaching the world, we overlook the basic fact that the fundamental way of reaching the world is to love your neighbor as yourself in the power of God. And many times, I'm afraid our local congregations go to great lengths to develop programs of various kinds, and I'm not attacking those. We need all of them, I'm sure. But we must include the rudimentary fact that we are able to love our neighbor as ourself, and in the power of God that takes care of everything. What we see today is too much of this being farmed out to what we think of as government agencies. But the widow and the orphan who are so often cited in the Bible cannot be helped adequately just by official sources. They need people to love them. And that's one of the great things that the Neighborhood Initiative does.

The Neighborhood Initiative is basically practical help in identifying and being with our neighbors. That's just the simple description of what happens. If a group goes down the street and finds someone who needs their house painted or something else like that, this is a ministry of love to our neighbors. And it is a way of reaching our communities that is a shockingly reversal of the isolation and loneliness in which many of our neighbors live. So often the widow and the orphan in our day is someone who has enough to eat but is starved in their soul and doesn't know that God loves them because it hasn't come to them through people who are around them.

So I say with tremendous gratitude, *praise God for the Neighborhood Initiative!* It is practical help in identifying and being with our neighbors. Who are they? How are they known? How do we contact them? The Neighborhood Initiative brings many, many suggestions as to how we can come to really deal with those with whom we are in close contact. The impact of this on our world will be overwhelming because it changes everything in the way we think about ourselves and the way we think about God. Where is God if He's not in our neighbor? And when He is in our neighbor, then He comes into our lives. Now our neighbor is simply someone with whom we are in close contact. But we have to recognize them and accept them as such. And the claim on us that comes when we recognize our neighbor is so great that it is frightening to many people, and they really don't want to get involved.

This is where we have to go back to the root of our lives in God Himself, and we have to believe that He will provide what we need as we do our best to provide for our neighbors and what they need. Our neighbors of course start very close. They are in our homes. Those are our first neighbors. And then perhaps the ones we work with, and the people who live nearby. Though in our world those are often very hard to reach because the old saying, "a man's home is his castle," is a saying that has taken on the force of having a moat around the house with alligators in it to keep people away. So the problem of breaking through that and coming to know your neighbor has implications that are difficult to overcome in our time. Nevertheless, it can be done with patience, and prayer, and watching, and a willingness to serve, and to know, and to be known. And that's essential to loving your neighbor as yourself.

Now who's to lead into this? The churches must be the leaders. And the pastors are the teachers. It is the churches alone that can make neighbor-love real in the power of God, *but we must intend to do that.* We have now quite a long history where failure to intend to do that has resulted in the kind of isolation that you often see even between Christians who are attending the same church. They're not really neighbors because they're not really involved in life with one another. Jesus, on the night before He was betrayed, says, "A new commandment I give to you, that you love one another" (John 13:34, NASB). Now that part of the commandment was not new. The part of the commandment that was new was what came next: "as I have loved you." And then Jesus goes on to say that the mark of His disciples is not that they have ripping good worship services or fantastic programs even for feeding the poor, as important as those may be. His mark was that the people in fellowship love one another, and that's what we need to cultivate. And that's the matrix out of which a community of neighbor-love then grows.

It is up to the pastors to stand and teach this. The pastors are to be the teachers of the nations.[1] They are the ones who have the knowledge from God. Knowledge of what is right and wrong and what is good and bad has now fallen away from our culture in general. It will not be recovered unless the pastors take their stand in their community as the teachers of their community. Now this may sound very audacious, but Jesus has assigned that role to us. We are to make disciples. We are to baptize them in the reality of the Trinitarian Community of Love and then teach them to do everything that He said. That is the solution to the human problem both for time and for eternity. It takes a special effort on the part of the pastor to assume that role.

There's a wonderful phrase that Paul uses in Romans 11:13, KJ21. Looking at the grace and ministry that had been given to him, he says, "I magnify my office." And I challenge every person, whether they're in the official role of a pastor or not, if they're a spokesperson for Christ, to magnify their office. And we may need to just take a moment here just to concentrate on that one thing: to magnify your office. . . . Perhaps you're the pastor of a small church, perhaps you don't even have a staff, or you're in some other ministry. What I'm saying to you is that the Neighborhood Initiative depends upon pastors magnifying their office as teachers of the nations, starting with the small group where they already have a voice.

"I magnify my office."

Pastors in our society are the only ones who have the position—and it may be small to begin with, or it may stay that way—but they have the position to do this. They have the content which is the precious teachings of the Bible, Jesus' teachings. I encourage you to go all the way back to the Ten Commandments and spend half an hour someday thinking about the difference that would be made if just the Ten Commandments were generally practiced as they have been at some times in our past. They have the power to make a difference. They have the position. They have the content. And they have the power. This is unique to the pastors. No one else has that. All you have to do is look at the various sources in government, education, and professional life and you will see that no one else has this. Only the pastors have it. And that's why they have their great responsibility in our world. Only they can overcome the problems that we have in our world today.

I also want to mention one thing about the moral problems in our society. The moral problems are rooted in character, and character is rooted in either the connection that we have with God or the disconnection. When we're out here trying to run our lives on our own in disconnection from God, that's where everything falls apart.

So my word today is: *We have the solution to the human problem*—the problem that's been there since Genesis, the third chapter. We have the solution to that. And we have to stand and present this solution in an incarnational form where it flows out from our fellowships through our fellowships, but out from our fellowships through the natural connections that people have in their lives in their world. If we do that, we will see the wonderful results that have been seen in the past as the people of Christ have stood as His disciples in this world, assuming the responsibility of love for their neighbors.

May God bless this all to you and make it real and powerful as you go forth to minister Christ to everyone you touch.

Dr. Dallas Willard
USC philosophy professor, author, speaker

Preface

Neighborhood ministry is not new to my wife, Jo, and me, as we have been opening our home for years. We learned a great deal in the 1970s about hospitality from Dr. Francis and Edith Schaeffer through their books and ministry at L'Abri in Huemoz, Switzerland. I also learned a great deal from the late Dr. Joe Aldrich, my professor at Talbot Seminary and neighborhood mentor. Joe told wonderful stories in class about caring for those in his Newport Beach neighborhood and his earlier years in an apartment complex while attending Dallas Seminary. In affluent and modest neighborhoods alike, Joe and his wife Ruthe took every opportunity to care for their neighbors. I am grateful to this prince of a man who modeled the love of Jesus to his neighbors.

Joe never would have imagined that what he was doing in his own neighborhood would one day sweep across our country and beyond. He simply obeyed Jesus' command to love his neighbor as himself. He was a true pioneer of what we now see happening in our land, and the legacy he left in my heart still spurs me on in my own neighborhood.

Acknowledgments

First and foremost, I want to acknowledge the Lord. Neighborhood Initiative (NI) is a part of what our Father is doing in our day. He has responded to the prayers of His saints and their appeal to Him to send out laborers into His harvest field.

I heartily appreciate my fellow pastors here in the San Fernando Valley who have labored faithfully in prayer for our city over the years; through their prayers, God introduced Neighborhood Initiative. I am also grateful to a group of advisors who gave me counsel, kept us all laughing in our meetings (sometimes at my expense), and believed enough in this good work to invest in NI with their churches and their counsel. These dear brothers include Dave Cuff, Dana Hanson, Dave Polus, Brian Cashman, Mike Cohen, Jeff Fischer, Brian Morehead, Eric Thomas, Daniel Gilbert, Chuck Smith, Jerry Moreno, Shah Afshar, Ken Crawford, Lyle Randles, and Rick McMichael.

I am grateful to those at the Valley Vineyard Christian Fellowship who have given themselves wholeheartedly and faithfully to Neighborhood Initiative since its inception. This is especially true of Martha Bellamy, Jan Enright, Anthony Rodriguez, Domingo Cabral, Roberto and Sharon Muñoz-Flores, Greg Stanley, Jim Johnson, Sharon Stone, Vivian Von Visger, Vicki Pistyur-Von Visger, Neftali and Deborah Santiago, Mike and Mary Day, Mary Alice Pollok, Maria Fischer, Elias and Ann Armenta, and all of the other wonderful people who continue to go outside the walls of our church to love their neighbors.

Neighborhood Initiative would have never come to be had it not been for neighbors in our community who responded to God's love and passed it on to other neighbors. The same is true of pastors like Andrew Burchett and Paul Haroutunian, who have taken the baton and passed it on to other pastors. May God's initiative continue.

I am grateful to my pastor, Bill Dwyer, for believing Neighborhood Initiative is a work of God, giving himself completely to this good work in his own neighborhood as well as others, and allowing me the freedom to devote time to this extensive project. I am blessed by Leroy Chavez, our worship pastor, for encouraging me with this project and helping me in so many ways through the years. I am indebted to Annette Grable, whose sifting through every word and comma of this book gave me the confidence to go public. And to Nadine Erickson, who has been a constant support and encouragement, whether serving and interceding in her neighborhood, designing work for NI, or rewriting what I have written. Also, I am grateful to Mary Makarios for her editing of portions of the early manuscript and Jarre Fees for her professional touch in making the book flow.

I thank God for connecting me with Kris Wallen at NavPress Ministry Services. She and her team took the ball when I didn't know what to do next and carried the book through to completion. Thanks for all of your outstanding help and wise counsel.

I am deeply thankful to Jane Willard for her amazing offer to include Dallas Willard's challenge in the book and to their daughter Becky Heatley for all her help to make Dallas's challenge a reality in video and in text.

I am most indebted to Jo Cory, my dear wife, who has modeled for me what it is to open our home to the church, our neighbors, missionaries, and perfect strangers. She is indeed my greatest blessing here on earth.

What Is Neighborhood Initiative?

*"The Whole Church Taking the Whole Gospel
to the Whole City, One Neighborhood at a Time"*

Simply stated, Neighborhood Initiative is the body of Christ at work in neighborhoods where God has placed us to bring about the transformation that comes through the power of His kingdom. Neighborhood Initiative is *not* a program, but a work that God is introducing to bring revival in His church and transformation to our cities. It's encouraging people to go out into their own neighborhoods to befriend their neighbors, open their homes, and lend a hand.

The seed of any plant has within its construct all that it requires to become what it will be at maturity. So like the tiny mustard seed, NI starts small in each of us and by God's power has the potential to change the culture of churches, relationships between churches, and the communities where we live. As God's kingdom work grows in us, and then through us, it will accomplish the construction of Christ's intended church, one of flesh that extends to the hearts outside our facilities and well-designed programs, meeting people where they are just as Christ did. If this appears to be a "method" or "program," which initially may seem systematic, I would say that is only because it may require a paradigm shift in our thinking about ministry.

Dallas Willard characterized Neighborhood Initiative in this way:

The great advantage of Neighborhood Initiative is that it provides a simple, accessible, and powerful way for every Christian to become involved in loving those around them with God-like agape love. Deeds of love toward others nearby is exactly the "washing of feet" that Jesus exemplified and told us to do. It recognizes and overcomes the alienation and aloneness that sickens our world and extends right into the heart of our congregations and nearby communities. It puts people first for Christ's sake, not church first. Discipleship to Christ is for the home, the streets, and the workplace. It is not a particularly religious thing, though specifically religious activities can also benefit from it as they in turn serve real life in our neighbors. Neighborhood Initiative is a primary way in which people of all kinds can "seek the kingdom of God and its kind of goodness" from where they are and as they are. They don't have to board the plane of religion after it is in the air.[2]

Chapter 1

How It All Started

Very truly I tell you, the Son can do nothing by himself; he can do only what he sees his Father doing, because whatever the Father does the Son also does.

John 5:19

Whenever I am asked to speak about Neighborhood Initiative, I first emphasize that it is not something I have authored or invented. To be perfectly honest, at the beginning of this road called NI, you will find skid marks where I was quite resistant to participating in what the Father was doing.

As a pastor, I have always been passionate about reaching those outside the church with the love of Jesus. My effort to get those in our church "outside" where Jesus spent His time has met some resistance. People have found it difficult to add one more commitment to their already demanding schedules. They may have agreed with my passion, but they were not moved to effective action. My own ingenuity was not enough. The door to Neighborhood Initiative gradually opened as I gave up my notions of how it should look. It was the Father's heart to reach those outside the church walls, but my passion for it had to come humbly alongside the work He had already authored and perfected. It took time for God to prepare me to understand what He was doing, and I think this is the constant tension for each of us, to continually humble our good intentions and our understanding to do His divine good will.

God has always been the initiator in reaching the lost. It is His work. Look at John 3:16, "For God so loved the world that he gave his one and only Son." He initiated this loving act from His throne in heaven. At the beginning of the church, Jesus said, "Do not leave Jerusalem, but wait for the gift my Father promised, which you have heard me speak about. . . . But you will receive power when the Holy Spirit comes on you; and you will be my witnesses in Jerusalem, and in all Judea and Samaria, and to the ends of the earth" (Acts 1:4,8). Being His witness requires the Spirit's power and direction. We see it so clearly throughout the book of Acts. If we live our lives in the world as Paul did, we must hear the Lord's voice, move out in His power, and take advantage of the opportunities that He creates.

Let me share my journey and how God initiated this good work.

Neighborhood Initiative Story

The roots of Neighborhood Initiative go back to October 4, 1997, when more than a million men gathered in Washington, D.C., for Stand in the Gap. Bill McCartney, former head football coach of the University of Colorado and then-head of Promise Keepers, called for a Sacred Assembly where we could humble ourselves before God. Our voices thundered throughout the National Mall as we sang out hymns of our faith in God. It is a sound I will never forget. We lay prostrate before our Lord, confessing our sins and asking Him to heal our land. It was a holy day in our nation's capital. At the close of this humbling day, Coach McCartney urged us to "Go back and win your city!" His exhortation resonated with me that day, as if God Himself was charging me with a directive for my own city.

Yet it was not until the year 2000 that I received any tangible direction. We as a church had gone through a very trying season, but because of God's faithfulness, He still revealed His will. A dear friend, Roberto Munoz-Flores, showed me the video series, *Transformations*, by George Otis Jr. The videos demonstrated the powerful work of God when people pray and intercede for a city. These compelling accounts gave me the direction I needed to take the next step.

On Friday, May 5, 2000, intercessors from our San Fernando Valley church gathered to pray for our city. We decided to meet the first Friday of every month at 10 p.m. to pray through the entire night. We found that praying all night was a challenge to even our most serious intercessors. I remember thinking during one of these all-night prayer gatherings, "Is this really accomplishing anything?" Dallas Willard encouraged us to "give it five years." This statement wasn't exactly encouraging, but we persevered. We prayed for local pastors and for God to move in our city through His church.

Chapter 2

The Long Wait

In January 2001, pastors in our Valley began to gather a couple of Thursdays every month to pray for our city. Soon we were gathering for weekly meetings. There has been opposition from our adversary at every advance, but we have persevered to this day. We set the following as our vision: to pray, to build relationships with one another, and to wait on the Lord to show us His plan for winning our city.

So we waited. And we waited. And finally, in 2007, LAPD Chaplain Ken Crawford initiated what was called Cleanup Los Angeles. The first cleanup was set for September of that year. I was asked to join with people from other local churches to participate in a cleanup in the LAPD's Foothill Division, located in the northeast San Fernando Valley. I was reluctant to participate, but I now see God's humor as He threw me onto the frontlines! I joined a team of students from California State University, Northridge (CSUN), led by then-CSUN Chaplain Kenny Farve. We went to Pacoima, where Kenny asked me to lead a team going door-to-door. The following week Ken Crawford included me in a meeting at a local restaurant where we evaluated the cleanup and dreamed a bit together about what God could do in the city through these efforts.

About a month later, we spent a Friday evening praying over some criminal hotspots in the city of Mission Hills in preparation for our next cleanup. More churches came on board, and we were able to accomplish a number of projects throughout the Valley. I marveled at what multiple churches could do together.

The Lord gave Ken a vision to start a pilot program called Adopt-A-Block to help churches take responsibility for the neighborhoods around their facilities. Ken selected some local pastors to participate and began to give us some direction. Prior to our second meeting, the Lord began to show me a way to launch Ken's program for our church.

During this time I was reading *The Externally Focused Church* by Rick Rusaw and Eric Swanson, who mentioned Tillie Burgin's work with Mission Arlington. At the Mission Arlington website, I was deeply moved by a video celebrating Tillie's twenty years of ministry. I saw that Mission Arlington was engaged in a powerful work of God. Mission Arlington helped to inspire Mission: Reseda, a project in which our church members adopted the eight square blocks around our church to care for as our own. God was showing me through Mission Arlington, and in a number of other ways, that He wanted us to be a part of a local mission in our own neighborhood. Our whole church had an opportunity to participate in a mission trip together—without the need for airline tickets, passports, or luggage. This was and is without question God's doing, and it has been an exciting venture.

The seeds of Mission: Reseda led to the fruit of what we now call Neighborhood Initiative. Today this vision moves the church from the safety net of church ministry to personally adopting neighborhoods where we live, and other churches in the Valley are beginning to do the same.

In January of 2011, my wife, Jo, and I were invited by our pastor friend Gus Gill to present a seminar for Denver pastors on what we had been doing in some of the neighborhoods in our Valley. I went with great enthusiasm to impart our treasured experiences but found myself leaving with more than I brought. Like my wife said to me at the airport after our stay in Denver, "They already had the meat and you just salted it."

There was such unity among the Denver pastors and a willingness to work together. They were encouraging their congregations to work together with other congregations in their neighborhoods. This opened my mind to the great possibilities with the pastors and congregations in our Valley.

In September 2011, we started a prayer meeting for pastors in our Valley who had a vision to reach neighborhoods in our city. We invited them to come together to pray for God's kingdom to break into our neighborhoods. Pastor Jeff Fischer from Hope Chapel took the lead in this new work. Jeff encouraged us to recognize that there is only one church in the Valley. He then challenged the pastors to adopt eight homes in their own neighborhoods and to learn the names of those who lived in each of those homes. He encouraged them to pray for those neighbors by name and to take an interest in their lives to see how each pastor might serve them. Jeff asked these pastors to invite other pastors to join us in prayer and in reaching our city through loving our neighbors.

There was great excitement in the air that morning when Pastor David Cuff from Calvary Chapel Mid Valley recalled with great passion what God had done over the eleven years that we had all prayed together. He pointed to the three purposes we had in coming together as pastors: to pray together, to develop relationships with other pastors, and to wait on God to show us what He wanted us to do in our city. David joked that he, a Calvary pastor, now had a strong friendship with Dana Hanson, a Lutheran pastor. "Calvary is afraid of everything," he said. He added that after all these years of prayer together, Neighborhood Initiative is what God wants us to do collectively as pastors in our city. It is what God wants those in our congregations to do together to bring God's kingdom to our city.

So after all these years, God had made His will known to us. I was reminded of what the apostle Paul said, "Make my joy complete by being like-minded, having the same love, being one in spirit and of one mind" (Philippians 2:2). When the leaders of the Lord's church in a city come together like this there is great joy within the Godhead, among the angels, and among His people.

This most certainly is what the Lord is doing in His church today. Walls are coming down. Pastors are acknowledging that there is but one church in the city, and they are under-shepherds; the Lord is the Chief Shepherd. May the Lord grant the pastors in your city the grace to work together to bring about revival in the churches in your city and awakening in the lives of those in your community.

Chapter 3

Ministry Begins at Home

Why the emphasis on neighborhood ministry? In addition to the fact that the Lord initiated this good work in neighborhoods, there are profound answers to this question that will show you how important it is to start where you live, to let your light shine in the neighborhood where God has placed you. He has placed you there for a purpose.

It's Natural and Authentic

Neighborhood ministry allows a church, or even those from different churches, to work together by moving outside the walls of the building to minister in the local community in a supernatural way.

For years I wanted to reach out to people in our city in a way that wasn't awkward, phony, forced, or even deceptive. While the different approaches were authentic and for the most part received a favorable response from strangers, they did nothing to build lasting relationships. It left me wanting something more. Loving your neighbors provides an avenue for relating to people in this way; after all, they are *our* neighbors. We see each other come and go and naturally share space and time together. Jesus commanded us to love our neighbors as ourselves. The simplicity of doing what He asks of us strips away all the unnatural methods and allows us to relate to people around us in a genuine and caring way. For the most part, those in our communities respond positively to this kind of love.

Days' Neighborhood

Mike and Mary Day, a couple from our church, are a perfect example of those expressing this kind of love. They have had a profound impact in their neighborhood, especially since embracing the concept of the Neighborhood Initiative. One neighbor said to Mike, "I've lived in this neighborhood for thirty-three years, and I have met more neighbors in these last two months than I have in all the years I've lived here."

Mike has initiated a number of things to encourage community. He has a prolific year-round garden on the side of his driveway and when the vegetables are ready to harvest, Mike takes his ripe produce up and down the street to share with his neighbors. His garden has become the center of attention for neighbors walking by and a means of developing friendships.

Mike and Mary recently threw a free car wash and barbecued hot dogs at their home for those in their neighborhood and those driving by. Many of their neighbors dropped by to talk and just hang out. After the first car wash, the neighbor across the street volunteered to host the next one. Other neighbors asked if they, too, could host a car wash. Car washes are an excellent way to involve neighborhood children, who are often isolated. These car washes have led to community dinners, barbecues, a neighborhood garage sale, and block parties.

Santiagos' Neighborhood

One day a team from our church joined Neftali and Deborah Santiago in their neighborhood for some extensive projects. The team trimmed two large mulberry trees that were hanging over the home of one of their new neighbors, hauled away large discarded items, washed cars, and built a fence. The neighbors were greatly impacted. The man whose trees were trimmed said that he couldn't afford to have them trimmed because all his savings went into buying a home in this neighborhood. He went on to say, "They never treated me this way where I used to live." He and his wife were incredibly grateful. Later, his wife told me that she'd shared the story at her job in a family-run business and everyone was surprised by this act of kindness.

One of my favorite stories from the Santiagos' neighborhood came a Sunday following one of our workdays there. An elderly woman named Joanne showed up at one of our church services and sat next to me in the front row just after the service started. She asked if she could tell everyone about her experience with what we were doing in the Santiago neighborhood. At first I was somewhat reticent, not knowing what to expect, but I threw caution to the wind and introduced Joanne as the Santiagos' neighbor.

She seemed very comfortable in front of everyone; her comments were moving and humorous. Joanne told the church how meaningful our visits to her home had been to her. She had experienced a family tragedy the year before and had been processing the grief with a counselor. The counselor had encouraged her to go to church around the time we showed up at her door. "What you are doing is working," Joanne said. "Don't stop."

Joanne's words that morning were an incredible encouragement to all of us. The Lord was pleased because the neighbors were experiencing His love through us. Doors were being opened for the gospel through genuine love and concern for people.

It Links Evangelistic Approaches

The question is often raised, why neighborhood ministry as opposed to any other approach to spreading the gospel? However, it is really not an approach per se, but rather a "context" for ministry that the church, for the most part, has neglected. In this context, Relational Evangelism, Servant Evangelism, Compassion Evangelism, Power

Evangelism, and Proclamation Evangelism can be bundled together and have the potential to bring the love of Christ to *every* needy person in a community. It also opens the door to hospitality, something that was quite prevalent in the early church.

In neighborhood ministry, each one of these forms of evangelism has been practiced with great success. Initially, relationship is established in the process of serving those in our neighborhoods. As we get to know them better and allow ourselves to be known, we become aware of deeper needs and can begin to pray and care for physical, emotional, social, and spiritual needs. It all happens so naturally.

Through my prior years of neighborhood ministry, I have found that neighbors are very observant and opinionated about each other. Aren't you? We usually have an opinion about each of our neighbors as assuredly as they have their opinions about us. When we choose to serve those in our neighborhood, these opinions often change.

Before Neftali started caring for those in his neighborhood, he didn't know his neighbors. In fact, as a man of African and Hispanic descent, he felt there might be some prejudice impeding any such relationship. It's impossible to say if those assessments were real or perceived, but in breaking through the obstacles to engage with his neighbors, those concerns disappeared. Several neighbors have now expressed a desire to elect Neftali mayor of their neighborhood, trusting him to be the representative for their entire community. Neftali recently said, "I used to go to our mailbox with my shirt off, but I don't feel comfortable doing that anymore." God not only transforms our neighbors, but uses them to transform our lives as well.

Chapter 4

Conspiracy of Kindness

Before we started Neighborhood Initiative, I was very involved in Servant Evangelism around our church facility. I had read Steve Sjogren's book *Conspiracy of Kindness* and organized a conference at our church for him to speak on that subject.

For one year, I spent an hour every Thursday afternoon with Jeff Morrison, a friend from our church, washing windshields in front of our local 7-Eleven and El Pollo Loco Restaurant. Cold weather or hot, we were there. Before we walked up the street we would gather our supplies and pray together, and then we would wash the windshield of anyone who would receive our offer. I have to say that it was always fun surprising people with this unexpected kind of love. They either wanted to pay us for our service or would ask us, "Why are you doing this?" Our simple answer was, "We just want to show you God's love in a practical way."

I have many stories from that year of washing windshields, but one stands out. I asked a woman if it would be okay to wash her windshield. I assured her I would do it for free and that there were no strings attached. She was visibly surprised by the request and she apprehensively accepted. As I was washing away, I sensed that someone inside El Pollo Loco was staring at me. I turned around to see the woman who had accepted looking at me in amazement. She motioned for me to come inside.

33

When I went in she said, "No one in this world would do what you are doing!" Much to my surprise, I responded, "I know, but I am not of this world." That is the beauty of Servant Evangelism: You can do something that is otherworldly. It is a beautiful expression of God's love demonstrated in such a simple way.

Though I enjoyed the weekly experience, I found that over the year of showing God's love in this simple way, something was lacking. I really never established lasting relationships with any of those whose windshields I washed, and this became a growing concern to me.

Taking Conspiracy of Kindness to the Neighborhood

As those in our church began to serve others in various neighborhoods, relationships naturally began to develop and we were able to see the impact these different acts of kindness had in their lives.

We observed how the Lord began to create unique opportunities for us in neighborhoods. We were experiencing God's presence as we served our neighbors, but we also began to know them and they began to know us. What started as an attempt to follow Christ's simple directive to love our neighbors drew us nearer to what our Father was doing.

As a friend recently said, "We are not looking to get people to sign on the dotted line, be saved, and move on to another lost soul. We are engaging in the process the Lord has already been invested in for someone's entire life—to love that person right where he or she is, allowing God to have His way, in His time."

Domingo Cabral's Neighborhood

On the very evening we first started Neighborhood Initiative, a representative from the Los Angeles Neighborhood Housing Services walked into our church and asked our senior pastor Bill Dwyer and me if we would be interested in participating with others in the community to paint five homes. The timing was remarkable, but the location of the five homes was even more so. Those homes were right in the neighborhoods that we were adopting. Approximately one hundred people from our church and two hundred from other service-oriented groups participated on that sunny day and the Lord used that activity to open up the hearts of neighbors in our community.

Domingo Cabral lived in one of those five homes. He came to the Lord while in prison, and he was looking for a church that did what Jesus did. He was taken aback by those from our church who showed him this kind of love, but he kept his distance to see if we were genuine. We told him we would help him trim his trees in the backyard, and when we followed through he began to realize that we were serious about being a presence in his community.

What also captured his attention was a young woman he saw walking through his neighborhood with her children. He wasn't sure what she was up to. Nadine Erickson, a woman from our church, made a practice of praying through Domingo's neighborhood. She took her four children on stroller rides through the streets and prayed for the neighbors. From those early days of prayer God has moved mightily in the neighborhood.

Within this neighborhood, we have hung Christmas lights, gone Christmas caroling, held major block parties, and had many free car washes. At one car wash, more than one hundred people participated. Two Mormon missionaries from Utah, who lived in the neighborhood, were very excited about the whole experience. One of them said to me, "This is the most exciting thing I've seen since I've been in L.A."

Domingo has since become very involved with our church and very committed to serving those in his neighborhood. He has painted the side of one neighbor's house, helped build a driveway gate for another neighbor, helped put in a new sidewalk for another, and done many other things for his neighbors because of the love

shown toward him. More importantly, he has developed meaningful relationships with many of his neighbors and has been there for
them when they needed someone. Domingo and I have become
best friends, and I was privileged to help him with a Bible study
for his neighbors at his local Starbucks.

Loving our neighbors brings together Relational and Servant
Evangelism. Both are very important forms of evangelism, but when
you naturally invoke them in the context of your own neighborhood, it confronts the common conception of who we are as
Christians. Many look at Christians through a veil of religion. But
Christ came to dwell in relationship with us, that *we*, bearing His
presence, would manifest that presence to others. All you have to do
is look for needs across the street or next door, take the initiative,
and the fun begins.

Each of us has something we can do to show the love of Jesus to
people just outside our door. This needn't be a full-time job or a
duty. Look at it rather as your own journey with Christ being made
public in your own community.

Chapter 5

Hospitality and Compassion

My wife and I now live in the nicest neighborhood we've ever lived in. Jo used to chase drug dealers off the corner across the street from our previous home. Our old neighborhood was riddled with gangs, and parolees living in apartments down the street, drive by shootings, and police helicopters flying overhead. The area was home for us for more than 20 years, but the thought of moving into a nicer neighborhood became very inviting to me.

When our family moved into Jo's parents' home, I was looking forward to living in a safer place. However, there are tradeoffs to living in a nicer neighborhood. It has been a little more difficult getting to know our neighbors. We have now lived in our new home for around fifteen years. We've had a number of events to cultivate relationships with our neighbors. I would like to say that we all are very close and spontaneously drop by each other's homes all the time, but that's not the case. However, there's good movement in that direction.

The greatest threat I have found to my ability to demonstrate love for my neighbors is a very busy schedule. One summer day, I came home from the office and said, "Jo, we need to say no to so many activities in our home." I had been so overwhelmed by the many things going on, from exchange students staying with us to an assortment of people coming and going, that I thought closing our doors was the best solution. It's not that these experiences weren't valuable. But like my involvement with Conspiracy of Kindness, those activities did not develop lasting relationships. If I had my way, I would spend my entire week with neighbors and family. This is my greatest passion as far as relationships, but time doesn't allow for it.

So when I told Jo that I was done with hosting so many activities, she responded, "I said yes to a baby shower here." "Whose baby shower?" I said. "Marcy's," she answered. "Marcy who?" I asked.

And Jo said, "Our neighbor." I stopped, completely speechless. That was exactly the kind of thing I'd been yearning for—activities that would allow me to practice neighborly love!

In retrospect, I did have too much going on. Being mindful about my time and energy is important, and it's imperative to listen to the Spirit so we are not so full of activity that we miss the golden opportunities He is preparing for us.

Sixteen women, many of them from the neighborhood, showed up for that shower. And just a few weeks after the baby shower, we hosted a Christmas dinner for our church small group. As people were arriving, I noticed that Jo was at the front door talking with Marcy.

Marcy's car had been broken into near her kids' school and her purse and a great deal of cash had been taken. She had to freeze her accounts at the bank, leaving her no easy access to emergency funds. Her husband was out of town on business and wouldn't be back until the following day. Here she was, just before Christmas, thirty-eight weeks pregnant and home alone with two young children. She was deeply concerned that whoever broke into her car, knowing that she had this amount of cash, would now be coming into our neighborhood, and she came to warn us. She was visibly shaken from the break-in and Jo asked if it would be okay if she prayed for her. Marcy agreed, and Jo put her hands on Marcy's shoulders and prayed. As Jo was praying, the Lord told me, in a way that only He can communicate, "Give her two hundred dollars."

After everyone had left our dinner party, Jo came up to me and said, "How much are we going to give Marcy?" I immediately responded, "The Lord told me two hundred dollars."

I had been to the ATM the day before and there was two hundred dollars in my wallet. I asked Jo to get a Christmas card ready and said I would go and see if Marcy was still awake. I took her the card with the gift inside.

The next day at the office, I got a call from Marcy. She thought I had given her just a Christmas card and she put it on her nightstand with all the others. She woke that morning and decided to read all of her Christmas cards, hoping to cheer herself up. After opening our card, she called in great surprise and said, "I will pay you back!" I said, "No, Marcy, that's a gift from God for you." Her response was priceless: "That's not normal!"

I love not being normal.

When I spoke to Marcy's husband the following week, he told me that when Marcy told him about the gift he "almost cried." I don't know how this all affected this couple in their relationship with God, but God knows their hearts and He is the One who will use this act of compassion to show them there is a God who loves them and cares deeply about what they are going through.

Mary Alice Pollok's Neighborhood

Depression is rampant in our cities and neighborhoods today. Left unchecked, it can lead people to consequences like suicide and even homicide. When believers who have the hope of eternity in their hearts reach out to troubled neighbors with compassion, terrible things like these can sometimes be prevented.

Mary Alice Pollok told me about an elderly neighbor across the hall from her apartment. "He and his wife are Jewish," she said. "When his wife passed away from cancer two years ago, he fell into a deep depression. I contacted the other neighbors that he and I knew, and for almost a year we took turns delivering dinners to him and checking on him. When his spirits would sink low, the kids and I would drag him out of his apartment and take him to the pool. One night, however, he fell into a serious depression and tried to kill himself with some pills. I called 911 and stayed with him until the paramedics got there. They took him to the hospital and saved his life.

"Afterward, he asked me why I cared so much about him when his own children did not even bother to keep in touch," Mary Alice said. "I was able to share that the love and compassion I have for people come from Jesus Christ. That is who he has seen in action over the last year and a half. This opened up many more conversations about life and death. With the Jewish faith there is no hope—but with Jesus, He is our hope. We run into each other weekly and he gives me updates on his progress."

Mary Alice had another experience with a different neighbor on the Fourth of July.

She had been at the community pool with her kids and was cleaning up after a barbecue they had shared with the neighbors. "It was just getting dark and we were getting our lawn chairs out to watch the Shepherd of the Hills (a local congregation) fireworks show," Mary Alice said, when she realized she had to make one more trip up to her third-story apartment.

She ran into a neighbor who hadn't been to the barbecue. Mary Alice invited her to watch the fireworks display and the neighbor declined. But Mary Alice "sensed the Holy Spirit beginning to move," and she insisted the woman join them.

"She did not leave my side for the next two hours," Mary Alice said. "When the [fireworks were] over, I offered to walk her back to her apartment. She agreed, and as we walked she confided in me that when she ran into me earlier, she had just returned from the store with enough over-the-counter medicine to commit suicide later that night."

The woman's fiancé had broken their engagement by phone

that morning, saying he had been with someone else for the past eight months. When she called her family in Iran to tell them, "they rejected her because she had moved out of the country to be with a 'foreigner.' Her grief was so great that she didn't think anyone cared whether she lived or died. She told me that the simple act of kindness that I showed her made her realize that someone did indeed care."

Mary Alice took that opportunity to share that the peace and joy she had in her life were from Jesus Christ. "She and I are now friends," Mary Alice said, "and I'm hoping that the seeds for her salvation that were planted that night will soon come to fruition. She is back on her feet and doing well."

Whether it's an acute need, chronic depression, loneliness, illness, or disability—whatever the need, we can be there for our neighbors to provide some measure of comfort or encouragement, and in some cases concrete assistance like providing cash or calling 911. We are to be like the Good Samaritan, to love our neighbors as ourselves. It was the religious people who didn't have time for the one in need. We are doing what Jesus would do if He lived in our neighborhoods.

Chapter 6

Doing What Jesus Did

Power Evangelism is God working through His people to bring about something they could not do on their own. Jesus even said to His disciples, before His crucifixion,

> I tell you, *whoever* believes in me will do the works I have been doing, and they will do even greater things than these, because I am going to the Father. And I will do whatever you ask in my name, so that the Father may be glorified in the Son. You may ask me for anything in my name, and I will do it.
>
> John 14:12-14, emphasis added

Jesus spent much of His public ministry healing the sick and practicing other supernatural activities. He invites us to carry on His public ministry by asking in His name for His kingdom to come and His will to be done. I have yet to find anyone who does His work perfectly, but as apprentices, He asks us to join Him by praying for the sick to be healed or anything that will bring His Father glory.

I have found that the Lord loves to answer these prayers. I try to take every opportunity I can to ask people if I can pray for them when they are in a difficult situation or have health problems. I am amazed how God responds. When I take the risk and ask someone if I can pray for him or her, even if it is at LA Fitness or for someone in our neighborhood, God responds to that kind of faith. The faith is not whether God can heal. The faith is whether I am willing to step out and ask people if I can pray for them if I notice or hear they have a need. Faith, as John Wimber used to say, is spelled R-I-S-K.

LA Fitness

While writing this section, two such opportunities came about. I play racquetball twice a week. I love the game, but even more than that, I enjoy the unique opportunities the Lord gives me to talk with other players and to pray for them.

A few weeks ago, some of us were about to play doubles. One of the guys was sitting on the floor with his hands over his eyes. He said he had "a terrible migraine coming on" and he couldn't open his eyes because it hurt too much. He got migraines three times a year, he said, "and they always last two days." I knew right away what the Lord wanted. I paused, mustered up my courage, and asked him if I could pray for him. Keep in mind, we were in the midst of other players outside the court. "Oh sure," he responded. After I finished praying I asked him how he was doing. He indicated there was no sign of relief. I said to him, "Now, if you get in your car and you are healed, come on back."

Two weeks later, I was getting ready to play another game of doubles, and guess who my partner was? Yes, this fellow with the migraine. He told me, "After you prayed for me, I went out to the car. As I was walking, I was afraid that I wouldn't be able to drive home because the migraine was so severe." But by the time he reached the car, he said, "the headache was completely gone."

The question is never whether I have enough faith for someone to be healed. It's about being obedient to pray when someone needs prayer.

The following week when I arrived at the courts, one of the regulars told me he wasn't playing because of a muscle spasm in his back. "I can play," he said, "but I don't want to injure it any more."

I thought, *I could say what I used to say: "That's too bad."*

Instead I asked, "Can I pray for you?" He was visibly taken aback by my request. He told me that he was in a deep search for God, studying the four major religions, and pointed out that the timing of my asking to pray for him was very significant. After I prayed for him I asked him how his back was doing and he said the pain was gone. We talked more and then he asked me if he could come to my church. I said, "Yes!" He pulled out a little piece of paper to write down all the information.

I was astounded by the experience. All I did was ask this guy if I could pray for a muscle spasm in his back. Then the Lord healed him and a door opened for this amazing conversation with him about my God. Jesus responds to these kinds of prayers so He can give His Father glory, and another person enters His kingdom. People who are seeking are especially ripe for such effectual encounters. My obedience was in line with God, who had already been sowing seeds in this man's life.

I believe this is what the Lord wants of us today: to take bold steps of faith in asking if we can pray for those in our communities as they have needs. He will respond and open amazing doors for us. We see this so clearly in Jesus' and Paul's ministries.

In Our Neighborhood

Once when I was talking to a neighbor, I noticed one of her arms was so discolored it was almost black. She had fallen into a rosebush and her arm was seriously infected from the thorns. She had chosen not to go to the doctor. I asked her if I could place my hand on her arm and pray for her, and she agreed. Weeks later, my wife and I stopped by her house and she thanked me for praying for her. She showed us her arm and said, "Look! It's all healed." I believe in my heart that God is pleased to heal in these unique situations.

These kinds of encounters with our neighbors show them there is a compassionate God who loves them, understands their pain, and wants to bring healing and restoration. These encounters wrestle with the notion so many people carry that God is angry, judgmental, and distant. We have the unique privilege of carrying on Jesus' ministry, which serves to nudge our neighbors closer to our loving God.

Proclamation Evangelism

When Jo and I were first married, we lived in an apartment complex. We intentionally got to know our neighbors and looked out for them. It was a friendly environment. Our building had a good mix of older and younger people. One of those neighbors, Don, took a liking to me. I was in my mid-twenties and he was sixty, which I thought was really old.

I invited him to church, and much to my surprise, he began to attend regularly. Once, at the back of our little chapel, he said to me, "I have been watching your life and I want what you have." I was quite surprised that a man of his age would humble himself to a man in his twenties. After a short explanation of the gospel, Don made a commitment to Christ.

Not long after this, Don asked if my pastor and I could come over and pray for his wife, Connie, who was Jewish. Connie had been diagnosed with terminal cancer and the doctors did not give her long to live. She could not even get out of bed on her own. My pastor and I joined Don in the living room of his apartment to pray for Connie. When we finished praying, Connie came bounding out of her bedroom yelling, "You did this to me! You did this to me!" And then she started doing jumping jacks in front of us. We were amazed! My pastor shared the gospel with her and she invited the Lord into her life.

A week later Connie slipped away into the presence of the Lord. Don asked if I would conduct a small memorial service for her in their apartment. We had a sweet gathering and many of those in the apartment building joined us to celebrate Connie's life. She had added so much life and laughter to our little community, and her presence was going to be missed.

When love and care thrive in a neighborhood, transformation of a community and the people within is inevitable.

Chapter 7

Set Up the Building Blocks

Once, I was collecting food in our neighborhood for our church's ministry to the poor. I put out flyers attached to grocery bags a few days before to alert our neighbors that I would be by to pick up their bags of food for those in need in our city. I was amazed that everyone who was home gave me at least one bag of food; others dropped off bags at our home. "You know why I give you these bags of food?" one neighbor asked. "It's because you are our neighbor and I trust you." When relationships are built in the neighborhood, trust is restored and community is revived.

We live in a time when fear and distrust generally rule in our cities and neighborhoods. I recently talked with a neighbor who lives near our church facility. As we talked together at Starbucks, he told me about an encounter he had in front of his home. As he was standing outside watering his lawn, some folks walked by and he greeted them warmly. He didn't get the warm response he had expected, but a look of fear that questioned his motivation.

It's sad that cities today have lost their sense of community. As I talk with people in our Valley and places around the country, I find that lack of community is becoming more and more evident. People don't know who to trust and assume that kindness is the means to sell them something. Even evangelism strikes the chord of manipulation, as if we are eager to push them into the kingdom before the Lord's timing.

Absentee parents, greed, television, the Internet, self-absorption, violence on the news, and so much more have all contributed to this decline. But many people actually want to know their neighbors, and want to be known in turn. More than once I have heard neighbors say they "always wanted to know" their neighbors and that they "had this back in my hometown growing up, but never here."

In his book *Making Room for Life*, Randy Frazee pointed out five things that make up the building blocks of community:

- Spontaneity
- Availability
- Frequency
- Common Meals
- Geography

An understanding of these building blocks of community became so apparent to me when we took a couple into our home for three months. The couple lived in northern California and moved here to be near UCLA Medical Center while the husband waited for a donor for a liver transplant. We welcomed them in and treated them like family. We didn't know them before they arrived at our home. We had dinners together, we spontaneously went to movies together, we talked with each other daily, and we were available for one another. This, in a nutshell, is community, and community must be nurtured and cultivated.

The practice of community has eroded from our neighborhoods today. There are many things that have contributed to this break-down, but I think there is a diabolical scheme to isolate us from one another. The church is isolated from the neighboring community and neighbors are isolated from each other. We drive into our garages or driveways, not to be seen again until it's time to go back to work or school the next day. I recently heard of one woman who had not talked to a neighbor in thirty years. This may be extreme, but there is something wrong with the way we relate—or do not relate—to each other in neighborhoods today.

Isolation inhibits community and is a logjam for the movement of God's kingdom in our cities. Isolationism cannot be countered with mere activity and definitely not by passing one another on our way to or from work.

Everybody's busy. But when we take a moment to be present with another person, we are breaking into dark places with light. Simply loving our neighbors can spark community in our neighborhoods again and provide the context for the spread of God's love.

Chapter 8

Shining Light into Darkness

t's a Wonderful Life is an all-time favorite Christmas movie. This film has captivated us for more than sixty years. I have family members who can quote lines from the movie word for word before they are spoken on-screen. But the closing scenes always grab me more than all the others.

When George Bailey realizes he is bankrupt and that Mr. Potter, the banker, finally has the upper hand, he drives to the outskirts of Bedford Falls intending to throw himself off a bridge. He finds Clarence, a guardian angel, thrashing in the water below. Instead of jumping to take his life, he jumps in to save Clarence's. Following this incident, George says to Clarence, "I wish I had never been born."

God grants that wish, and Clarence shows George what the town of Bedford Falls, now called Pottersville, would be like if George had never been there. George, in the closing scenes, becomes aware of what he has meant to the community and what a wonderful life he has had.

Today our city, like many other cities in the United States, is corrupt. Our Valley is infamous for being the porn capital of the world. We would put Pottersville to shame. For some reason we don't see our city the way George did. Perhaps we are desensitized to its condition. Maybe we assume that because we don't know how to battle the darkness, it's easier to ignore it or leave it for someone else to address. Dallas Willard said, "There is only one responsible party."[3] And it's not the absence of George Bailey; it's the absence of the church.

Things may have gotten worse in modern times, but moral degradation in our cities is not a new problem. Jesus told us what it would take to turn our cities around and how crucial the church is to any community in bringing about moral and spiritual transformation. "The kingdom of heaven is like yeast that a woman took and mixed into about sixty pounds of flour," Jesus said, "until it worked all through the dough" (Matthew 13:33).

Yeast is a living organism that forms colonies of single, simple cells. When a small amount is kneaded into flour and water it will eventually infuse and cause the dough to rise. Like yeast does in flour, God's kingdom has the potential to transform a community. However, like yeast that does not infuse, if the kingdom of God does not permeate communities where we live, we are left with cities that look like Pottersville — cities that have lost their way. We who know and love Jesus are agents of God's kingdom. We represent those living cells that God wants to work into our neighborhoods to permeate the malevolence in our cities.

In Matthew 5:14, Jesus calls us "the light of the world." We're it! There is no plan B. But our adversary the Devil has done a masterful job of isolating the church from the world, keeping the light of God's kingdom from penetrating the darkness in which we all live. He is quite content to have us fill our time and calendars with church activities because it keeps us busy while a lost world plunges into deeper darkness. Jesus came to shine a light on that darkness, essentially partnering with us in this life.

Jesus encourages us in Matthew 5:15-16 not to hide our light, but to let it shine before men, so they will see our good works and glorify our Father in heaven. I am convinced there are two ways to hide our light. One is to retreat from the world and the other is to become so adept at living in it that no one can tell us apart from those in the world.

In the book *The Externally Focused Church*, Rick Rusaw and Eric Swanson make this point about externally focused churches, "They don't shout at the dirty stream; they get in the water and begin cleaning it up."[4]

There's no better place to start than the neighborhoods where we live, and then to work our way out from there. I strongly believe if we who are in the church see our homes and neighborhoods as the center for ministry, we will begin to influence the cities where we live. Our influence begins where we live and will be felt wherever we go. Start with your own Jerusalem and let it spread. You will turn your world upside down.

Chapter 9

Side by Side,
All Over the Country

Over the years, local congregations have seldom worked together, unless there was an evangelistic crusade or a catastrophe that forced a cooperative response. It's exciting to see walls between pastors coming down and a growing camaraderie among church leaders rising up. Pastors are bringing their congregations together with other churches for common worship services and working together in community efforts in their cities.

In January 2009, a group of Denver pastors came together to dream about what it would look like to join their congregations to make a difference in their communities. It took a while, but for three weeks in the month of May 2011, forty-four of those pastors preached on subjects related to loving your neighbor. They challenged their congregations to sign up at the Art of Neighboring website and commit to getting to know eight neighbors. Around three thousand people signed up. The pastors asked them to join with those from nearby congregations to reach out in love to their neighbors. They suggested starting with a block party and offered website resources for organizing one. You can read and hear their stories at www.artofneighboring.com.

When I adopted those in my present neighborhood, they began to tell me about other neighbors and their church background. Out of the thirty-four homes that I adopted, three people including me were pastors, and eleven homes were part of different congregations. As I walked and prayed for my neighbors, I would think, "Wouldn't it be wonderful if all those from different churches worked together in our neighborhood to love our actual neighbors as ourselves?"

That thought has never left me. And now that I'm seeing what's happening in Denver and in our Valley, I believe this could become a reality. Can you imagine if neighborhoods across America and around the world began to work together in the common cause of the Great Commandment, "Love your neighbor as yourself," and the Great Commission, "Go and make disciples of all nations"?

Chapter 10

Sowing the Seeds

Our congregation meets in the San Fernando Valley, home to nearly two million people. I asked a class I was leading one Wednesday evening, "If you were a farmer and you were given the responsibility of planting and gathering a harvest out of every area of our Valley, how would you go about it?" The answer was pretty simple. The participants said they would break up the Valley into smaller sections and assign farmers to each section. Each farmer would plant seeds in his field and before long a harvest could be gathered from every field across the Valley.

Consider the spiritual implications of this response and what Jesus had in mind when He said, "The harvest is plentiful but the workers are few. Ask the Lord of the harvest, therefore, to send out workers into his harvest field" (Matthew 9: 37-38).

The Lord of the harvest is asking us to work in a section of His harvest field. Picture the Midwest and its sprawling farmland. Don't you generally find a farmer's home in or near each field? The Lord has situated His people in homes so we can work in the field He has assigned to us.

As the Lord was opening my eyes to the Neighborhood Initiative, I remember driving almost weekly to be with my elderly father. I would leave our suburban street and take the back road to spend the day with him in a nearby city. As I made the trip, I would admire the beauty of the farmers' green fields that had been cultivated and cared for. I saw the systematic work of those who worked in the fields. It wasn't haphazard because it was their intention that a harvest would come from every section of the field. I remember thinking, *Why has it not occurred to the church to take such care of our own neighborhoods? Couldn't we work systematically in neighborhoods throughout our area just as those farmers do?*

As I made those trips during that season, I realized we really can't understand the agricultural parables of the New Testament as they were intended until we see them from a farmer's perspective. Most of us in the church today live in urban or suburban settings and can't really appreciate the significance of why Jesus used this imagery. He used it with His disciples because they were extremely familiar with it and it best explained the kind of work that they were entering into within the context of their communities.

If we can learn to view those in our neighborhoods as the field that the Lord has given us to carefully cultivate, then like the farmer, we could better understand the ministry the Lord had in mind for His church.

What we see taking place in Denver, our Valley, and across our country has the potential to fulfill the Lord's directive to work in His harvest field. Just like the farmer, we can cultivate and care for the field assigned to us, allowing the Lord to draw the harvest from each of our neighborhoods, in each of our cities, in His time. Our job is but to plant and tend the crops around us, mindful that our efforts belong to the Lord.

Chapter 11

A Simple Plan

The direction Jesus gave His disciples should help us understand the importance of neighborhood ministry: "Whatever town or village you enter, search there for some worthy person and stay at their house until you leave. As you enter the home, give it your greeting. If the home is deserving, let your peace rest on it; if it is not, let your peace return to you. If anyone will not welcome you or listen to your words, leave that home or town and shake the dust off your feet" (Matthew 10:11-14).

In the Scriptures, Jesus is not only giving a directive for the twelve disciples (and later the seventy), but also establishing a precedent for His church in the spread of the gospel and His kingdom. We see throughout the book of Acts how the disciples followed His plan, bringing in a tremendous harvest for their labor.

There are other contexts through which the gospel will spread; however, in Jesus' directives to the disciples the context for the advance of God's kingdom is through the unique Christian home. He instructs them to go to a town or village and find a "worthy person" and stay at his house.

The home was to be the center for ministry and the movement of the gospel. The disciples recognized that they were *all* a part of an exciting movement initiated by the Lord Himself. The kingdom of God was on the move and believers wanted to join in and see the world transformed. We see this so clearly in Paul's ministry. It was said of Paul and others in Acts 17 that they "turned the world upside down" (verse 6, KJV).

There is another by-product to the home-based model. I notice that often the children of those steeped in ministry do not grow up to embrace the convictions of their parents and in many cases leave the faith altogether. When ministry moves from the church building to the home, we are forced to reckon with the real state of that home. We tend to engage just enough to allow God room in those relationships within our home, without allowing Him to *dwell with us*. It is here that true discipleship can take place within our families as well as with our neighbors.

As we see at the inception of the church, the young disciples weren't satisfied with just gathering with believers. They moved outside of their close-knit community and engaged others everywhere in the city of Jerusalem. The result, according to Acts 2:47, was that they enjoyed the favor of all the people and the Lord added to their numbers day by day. When we demonstrate the life of Christ in and out of our front door—I mean the messy, real walk of faith—then we have a much more diverse audience than we would ever get in church.

Have you ever wondered why the modern church doesn't look like the early church, the one in the book of Acts? For that matter, why doesn't our ministry today look like Jesus' ministry? You could say it was primitive then and life was simpler, and that now the church is more sophisticated with its buildings, structure, and programs.

How's that working for us? Is the church growing as it did during the first three centuries of its existence? Perhaps it is growing in parts of the world, but not in the United States. One prominent reason the church today does not look like the church in the book of Acts or like Jesus' ministry is that the home does not exist as the center for ministry. We have made the church building the center for ministry, and that leaves us with an impotent church. We are not reproductive. We're satisfied with *adding* people to our buildings, but not *making and multiplying* disciples.

Paul made a case for this in Acts 20: "You know that I have not hesitated to preach anything that would be helpful to you but have taught you publicly and from *house* to *house*" (verse 20, emphasis added). There were public settings for the proclamation of the gospel, but the movement spread from house to house.

The church facility today is a primary place for believers to grow and learn. But it's what we do with those lessons after we leave church gatherings that matters. Real sacrifice of self is guaranteed to come to your table as you transparently walk out the journey of relationship with Christ in the midst of your home and city.

It's not that I'm opposed to buildings. But if buildings stand in the way of the advancement of God's kingdom, community, priority of family life, or city transformation; if they become a fortress to hide behind and protect us from the outside world; or if they create exclusiveness, then I am certainly opposed to them. Jesus sent His disciples out as sheep among wolves, and that directive for His church has not changed. He sent them out to find people of peace, stay in their homes, and make disciples, because He knew that's how the gospel would spread.

In *Evangelism in the Early Church*, Michael Green points out that those early leaders had a strategy: "Christian missionaries made a deliberate point of gaining whatever households they could as lighthouses, so to speak, from which the gospel could illuminate the surrounding darkness."[5] He points out that the early church stressed the centrality of the household for the advancement of Christianity.

Rodney Stark's book *The Rise of Christianity*[6] charts the exponential growth of the church during the first three centuries:

Christian Growth Projected at 40 Percent per Decade

Year	Number of Christians	Percent of Population*
40	1,000	0.0017
50	1,400	0.0023
100	7,530	0.0126
150	40,496	0.07
200	217,795	0.36
250	1,171,356	1.9
300	6,299,832	10.5
350	33,882,008	56.5

* Based on an estimated population of 60 million.

Early Christians accomplished this by following the simple plan that Jesus gave to His first disciples.

Chapter 12

The Home-Centered Ministry

Jesus had a plan for home-centered ministry, and it's as applicable today as it was two thousand years ago.

1. Look for "People Who Welcome You."

Jesus directed His disciples to go into communities and look for those in neighborhoods who would welcome them, literally, into their homes. But in addition to being received, it also means that those in the home should receive the disciple's teaching. Jesus clarifies this when He tells His disciples, "Whoever listens to you listens to me; whoever rejects you rejects me; but whoever rejects me rejects him who sent me" (Luke 10:16).

Understanding what Jesus is saying here is so freeing for us today as we work to spread the gospel. So often we feel the burden is on us to make people like us and to arm-twist them into receiving the message of the gospel, when the exact opposite is true. Jesus puts the responsibility on the recipient to become a seeker of truth.

It is up to the recipients to welcome us. They may be attracted to something in us (Jesus) and desire what we have. Perhaps they have been thinking about spiritual things for some time and will be drawn to you without knowing why. They may say something like, "You have a peace about you," or, "I like your family. You seem so different." They might even say, "I like you," or, "I like being with you." Whatever it is, they will take a liking to you. These are signs of a welcoming person.

2. Look for a "Worthy Person."

Why does Jesus refer to someone as a "worthy person"? I asked myself this question many times, but it wasn't until I stumbled across a section in Acts 13 that it became clear to me.

When the apostle Paul was in Pisidian Antioch, he preached the good news in the synagogue on the Sabbath. He and his message were received with great favor. On the next Sabbath, almost the whole city gathered to hear the Word of the Lord from him. However, there were Jews in the city who were jealous and talked abusively against Paul and against what he was saying. In response, Paul and Barnabas said to them: "We had to speak the word of God to you first. Since you reject it and do not consider yourselves *worthy* of eternal life, we now turn to the Gentiles" (Acts 13:46, emphasis added).

What makes one "worthy" is a receptive heart to the message of the gospel. Note the accessible hearts of the Gentiles when Paul speaks to them: "When the Gentiles heard this, they were glad and honored the word of the Lord; and all who were appointed for eternal life believed" (Acts 13:48). Worthiness is not about anything we do, but about being responsive to what Jesus has said and done on our behalf.

3. Look for People of Peace.

Like the worthy person, the person of peace is someone who is receptive to you and the gospel. However, there is a little twist here that sheds light on why this person is receptive. The term "person of peace" implies that the worthy person's heart has been prepared and is open to Jesus and the gospel.

In an interview with *Christianity Today*, Jerry Root said, "I've sensed that evangelism is not something we do in isolation from God. We don't take him to anybody—he's already there and already more interested in that person than we are, and somehow engaged with that person. We're not just speaking the gospel to an uninterested audience."[7]

The person of peace is someone to whom God has been speaking and preparing for an encounter with one of Jesus' disciples. We see this clearly in Acts 10 when God links Cornelius with Peter. He speaks first to Cornelius through an angel in a vision, and then Peter receives a vision as well. Later, a voice instructs Peter to meet Cornelius, a Gentile and someone with whom Peter would never have associated. The Spirit of the Lord speaks to Peter, thereby setting up a remarkable encounter with a man of peace.

Because God had already been at work in his life, Cornelius was receptive to the message of the Lord through Peter. In fact, Cornelius's whole household responded to Peter's message and was baptized.

A person who receives God's peace has had an encounter that prepares him for salvation and discipleship. God's peace rests on him because God's favor is with him; as it says in Luke 2:14, "On earth peace to those on whom his favor rests." Upon encountering those who have received this anointing, Jesus instructs His disciples, "When you enter a house, first say, 'Peace to this house.' If someone who promotes peace is there, your peace will rest on them; if not, it will return to you" (Luke 10:5-6). Two things are sure: There are those who will be receptive and those who will not. Jesus tells us what our response should be with each of them. In the next two sections we will examine our response to these two types of individuals.

4. If They Are Not Responsive, Move On!

"If anyone will not welcome you or listen to your words, leave that home or town and shake the dust off your feet" (Matthew 10:14). These words seem harsh and heartless. Jesus' encounter with the Rich Young Ruler gives us a behind the scenes understanding of this instruction. When the young man chose to walk away after Jesus' directive to sell all he had and give to the poor, the Lord did not try to coerce him to follow through with His directive. Jesus gave him the freedom to make his own choice.

We too want to honor people's choices and devote our time to those who welcome us. In the future, the Lord may use those who are responsive to us and the message of the gospel to reach those who rejected us and our message the first time.

5. Stay with the Person of Peace.

Jesus says, "Stay in that house" (Luke 10:7, NASB). Once you have found a person of peace, devote time to the relationship. Remember Jesus' encounter with the woman at the well (see John 4). Jesus took time to patiently and graciously reveal who He was and then she went back and told everyone she knew. She eventually became the link to winning those in the city of Sychar. It has been said, "If you find gold, there may be a vein." Peter found gold in Cornelius, and he was the instrument God used to reach his whole household. Likewise, the woman at the well was the means to reaching her city.

I was introduced to the Lord while in Thailand during the Vietnam War. Dave McNeal and I were combat motion picture cameramen in the Air Force. He worked as a volunteer with The Navigators, an international, interdenominational Christian ministry, and devoted six months to building a relationship with me, sharing the gospel, helping me understand and apply the Scriptures to my life, and making sure I found a good church when I returned to the States.

For years I thought he spent too much time with me when he could have devoted time to making the gospel known to so many more. However, Dave was following the Lord's instruction to "Stay in that house"; he stayed with the person of peace and devoted precious, meaningful time to the person whose heart was receptive to Jesus. I am like the woman at the well. I had my means of gold. Those six months sowed deeply into my walk with Christ and have been well worth Dave's investment.

Chapter 13

Boldness and Benefits

When the home becomes the center for ministry, everyone benefits. Jesus established the home as the center for ministry from the very onset of the church. Moving into home-centered ministry requires a boldness that may meet with resistance, but the benefits cannot be denied.

Home and Family

- It makes home and family life the center again.
- It revives hospitality in the homes of believers.
- Community among believers is enhanced.

Neighbors

- We are no longer seen as "church people," but as neighbors.
- Everyone can be systematically touched with the love of Jesus.
- Neighbors experience community, and neighborly love fills the community.
- We no longer see the neighbors as a project, but as people sojourning alongside us.

Church

- Everyone in the church gets to play in the game, and we lose the Sunday spectator mentality.

- Church is not a Sunday-only thing but active 24/7.
- The church moves away from the club mentality and into a caring community for those in the city.
- Home groups/community groups/house churches (whatever you want to call them) take priority over programs and activities in the building.
- The church has unbelieving friends.
- Relationships with those outside the church form naturally, rather than through church-related programs.
- It's not another program that will die out.
- We can't walk away from our ministry.
- People from different congregations can work together in their own neighborhoods.
- The church is revived and becomes involved in a movement of God.

City

- We bring community life back to our cities.
- The city takes priority and benefits in multiple ways (when we become salt and light in the community): impeding crime; caring for the needs of the poor, the homeless, and the addicted.
- We gain favor with local government.
- The church becomes the servant of the city.
- Awakening of God comes to our cities.

Advancement of God's Kingdom

- There is potential for exponential growth—the bigger it gets, the faster it grows.
- When a neighbor becomes a disciple, follow-up is much easier, because he or she lives just down the street.
- What might take hours to do in preparation for typical ministry can occur in the natural space of going about the day.

- When neighbors come to faith they become an extension of the love they have received and in turn share that love and joy with other neighbors.
- The church moves away from a focus on bigger buildings and becomes committed to the Great Commandment and the Great Commission.

The Art of Neighboring website captures the heart of loving your neighbor in this statement:

We are a group of people who are discovering that Jesus is actually a genius. When he was asked to reduce everything to one command, he gave us a simple strategic plan that if every believer actually did . . . would literally change the world. This simple plan also offers us a different kind of life. Whenever we center our lives around the Great Commandment, and take very literally the idea and practice of loving our neighbor, there's great freedom, peace, and depth of relationship that comes to our lives. By becoming good neighbors, we're stretched and shaped and become who we're supposed to be. And our communities become places that draw others to God.[8]

Chapter 14

The Church Becomes Missional

What is being introduced is an entirely new paradigm for church life. If the church follows through with Neighborhood Initiative, current church culture will profoundly change. It will first change churches individually and then corporately throughout cities. Churches will see that they need one another to carry out the mission of bringing the whole gospel to the whole city. It is a welcome change, but there will be resistance by some to moving away from familiar or traditional approaches.

Churches will become missional, a trait that is missing in the American church today. American churches rely most on transfer growth to increase the size of their congregations. It states in the description of *Grow Your Church from the Outside In* by George Barna, "More than 80% of the current growth registered by Protestant churches is biological or transfer growth—very little of the growth comes from penetrating the ranks of the unchurched."[9]

If a congregation has a dynamic pastor and a large staff, or has very attractive facilities and programs for everyone, then those from smaller congregations are drawn to it. On the other hand, some leave the larger church because they want something smaller, more like a family. Whatever reasons people have for changing churches, this movement has not helped to expand Christ's kingdom here in the United States.

Recently two missionaries read and responded to our Neighborhood Initiative material. One said, "This is what missionaries do." The second said, "This is what we did in Tajikistan," where transfer growth doesn't work because there are no other churches from which to draw. For six years this missionary and his family went out and met their neighbors, had block parties, established relationships with them, served them, cared for them, and prayed for them, until the Lord opened a door for the gospel.

The church in America is in decline simply because it is impotent. We are not making disciples. We have invested so much of our time with those in the church that we have little time left for those outside the church. As a result, we have lost touch with our culture, we have become marginalized and trivialized, and we have very little influence. We need to "do what missionaries do."

The Lord is moving the whole church to become missional. As we might expect, there will be resistance because it is easy and comfortable to continue doing what we have always done. However, if we accept the challenge of making the home the center for ministry and follow Jesus' simple plan of allowing the Holy Spirit to lead us into what the Father is doing, we will experience what we've read about in the book of Acts. We will gradually begin to hear of God's kingdom breaking into neighborhoods, apartments, campuses, workplaces, and cities.

The Lord is already awakening His disciples to this commission, and as a result we are seeing the Lord bless our understanding of it. I believe what's coming is an awakening in our city like we have never seen before.

Chapter 15

The Church's New Frontier

The Word became flesh and blood, and moved into the neighborhood.

John 1:14, MSG

How do you develop a neighborhood ministry? Very simply, you start by becoming a good neighbor. You commit yourself to loving your neighbor as yourself and, led by the Spirit, showing him or her this kind of love.

Look for what God is doing in your neighborhood already and join Him in His work. Your motive is quite pure. You want to love those in your neighborhood and only do what your Father is doing. He is the One who will initiate and open doors and then invite you to step into the opportunities He creates for you. Unlike a job that has set functions, your role in your neighborhood will vary from day to day. You may find yourself being a caretaker, a friend who listens, or a prayer warrior standing in the gap for your neighbor.

I remember when I decided to become a good neighbor to those in our present neighborhood. I began early morning prayer walks past the homes of those in our neighborhood whom I felt God had specifically called me to love. Once I made this commitment to my neighbors, a dramatic shift occurred in my thinking and I began to reinhabit my neighborhood emotionally.

Over the years, Jo and I have organized a variety of activities for our neighbors, but this was different. I now saw these same people as those for whom God was asking me to care, those for whom Christ died. I now cared more deeply about them and what they were going through in life.

On July 4, 2009, I was painting some woodwork when I heard a fire truck and ambulance race by our home and into *my* cul-de-sac (emphasis on "my" because these are the ones I pray for). I quickly changed out of my paint clothes and ran up the street. The paramedics were carrying my neighbor Jim out of his house on a stretcher. I found his wife Paula, comforted her, and offered a one-sentence prayer before they left in the ambulance. In the past, I wouldn't have gotten involved, but now they were more than strangers living down the street.

A few days later on my early morning prayer walk, I was surprised to find Jim sitting by his open window. He seemed fine, and we talked a bit. Jim told me that he had an aneurysm and surgery was scheduled for the following week. But that was to be our last conversation because Jim passed away soon after.

I had met him through one of the free car washes at our home several years earlier. Jim had been a devout atheist, but was very sympathetic toward Christians because he felt we were mistreated. He had wanted to create a website called "Atheists for God." I know what you are thinking, and I agree. We had many conversations over the years. After Jim's passing Paula asked if I would officiate at a celebration of Jim's life. Paula guessed that fifteen people would attend, and I offered to host the event in our home.

My wife handed out invitations to the neighbors a few days before the service. We were pleasantly surprised by all the family, friends, and neighbors who attended. Well over the expected fifteen people showed up! Our living room was filled to overflowing, and it was standing room only in our adjoining dining room. People shared their memories of Jim, and it was truly a celebration of his life. At the close, I had an opportunity to talk about why funerals and memorial services are significant as recorded in Ecclesiastes 7, and most importantly about the Resurrection. It's one thing to share these kinds of things with church people or people you don't know, but quite another with your neighbors. It was a remarkable experience. God opened this door, and all I had to do was walk through it.

Even though he called himself an atheist, Jim was easier to reach than some. But what about the really difficult neighbors?

The Hard Cases

The general response to NI from people in our congregation as well as other pastors has been very favorable. But some people have said, "My neighbors are so difficult. Nothing could ever happen in our neighborhood!"

I listen quietly when this happens and try not to offer trite solutions when people say how impossible it would be to show this kind of love to their neighbors. I commit to pray for them and those in their neighborhood. Why? Only God can make a difference in their neighbors' lives. Only God can create opportunities that turn things around in a neighborhood. Yes, we can do unconditional acts of kindness that may help with difficult neighbors, but it's God who changes hearts and knows the hidden keys to unlock relationships.

Pastor Dave's Neighbor

Dave Cuff is a dear friend of mine. The first time I talked with him about reaching out, I had a feeling this "neighborhood thing" wasn't for him, not realizing that he had been attempting to love a particular neighbor for some time. But one Thursday morning at our weekly pastors' prayer gathering, Dave shared this story. "I met Tom ten years ago right after I moved in next door to him," Dave said. "He told me he had been an alcoholic for more than forty years and had been sober for the last two months.

"A few weeks later I was taking out my trash early in the morning and noticed many undercover law enforcement vehicles in front of my house. They all got out of their vehicles at once and before I knew what was happening they had Tom in handcuffs on his front lawn. It turns out they were serving a warrant for one of Tom's prior room- mates. But when they asked me what I knew about Tom I remember saying he was a nice neighbor and a sober alcoholic.

"Over the years we have had a friendly and casual relationship," Dave said. "Over the next ten years Alcoholics Anonymous became his life. Our church reached out to him by helping with his house projects, and I mowed and edged his lawns often. I shared the gospel with him many times, and he was always respectively positive but never had time to pray with me or come to church."

Then Tom was diagnosed with liver cancer.

"I remember the first day he told me about it," Dave said, "because he said it was his own fault for drinking for over forty years and he didn't blame anyone. We prayed . . . and after his surgery it seemed he was going to make it. He came over more often and our relationship took a more personal and sensitive turn.

"Then his liver cancer returned and the doctor gave him two months to live. I remember making a point to spend more time with him when he told me. We invited Tom and his girlfriend of twenty years over for dinner and a swim. My family really made a special time for them. We went swimming and had dinner and des- sert. Jim loved to go to the movies, so I took him to see *The Avengers*.

"I remember the feeling I had before taking him to the movies was one of pressure to share the gospel again," Dave said, "but also just wanting to show him a great time. My wife said that he would probably bring it up, and before my car left the driveway he did. We had a great time and Jim said he was ready to meet Jesus. . . . Two weeks later he died. My only regret is that I did not spend more time with him over the last ten years."

The video of Dave sharing this story is at http://neighborhood initiative.com.

I like to believe that God can do this kind of thing in every neighborhood, even if it seems impossible. Our tendency is to think nothing will change, but as we see in Tom's case, a dramatic change in life can change people's perspective. They need only welcome you, and you need only give them time and show them God's love.

There are exceptions. Sometimes neighbors make it evident that they would be happy to see you move out of "their" neighborhood. That was the Carters' experience.

The Carters' Dearing Street Neighborhood

Mike and Cindy Carter served as missionaries from our church for at least two years on the mission field in Baja, Mexico, with a wonderful agency called Foundation for His Ministry. In addition to working at the mission, they were also very involved with those in the local community. They are incarnational people. When they moved back to their home here in the San Fernando Valley, they attempted to carry on their work in their neighborhood. However, they met real resistance from some of their neighbors. After I spoke on "Being the Light of the World in 2013", Cindy e-mailed me her neighborhood concerns.

"Over the last fifteen years in this house, we've tried hard to make a community," she wrote. "A few weeks before Christmas, I had the 'Women of Dearing' over for tea/breakfast. It was beautiful to see a kind of neighborly friendship/familiarity between several of us women. But as I listened to your message, I felt a nudging to go further. Be the light.

"'Don't just be nice'—which honestly in this neighborhood is really a challenge," she went on. "I have one neighbor who plays his music as loud as possible every time we have a backyard gathering. I have another who has [a lot of people] living in his house, and they all park their cars in front of our house so we never have a place to park.

"Another neighbor has a Chihuahua that's left out on the

balcony barking 24/7, and a different neighbor who has five barking dogs in her yard. These are all the people just in the houses next to us! There are a lot more issues—like gangs and drugs—going on farther up and down the street. And in all of these situations, I have had to be the 'complaining' neighbor at some point. I'm sure they don't see us as the beacon of hope. They may see me as the neighborhood trouble-maker/whiner! I'm praying about how to take it to the next level. How can I move from 'order-keeper' to 'light of Dearing'?"

Cindy's e-mail went on to say that she had "kind of given up" and was tempted to move, or bury her head.

"But after your message," she wrote, "I feel a renewal to pray and try again. At least people know who we are! Oh Lord! Give us vision and hope for the neighbors on Dearing!"

Cindy is a very real person, and that's one of many reasons people in our church really like her. I like her willingness to go for it even though the situation seems bleak. After talking with her, I assured her I would be praying for her and her family and that God would move in her neighbors' lives. It meant a lot to her that I would be praying, and I look forward to seeing what God will do.

Chapter 16

The Five Essentials

Before you move out into your neighborhood, whether you have one like the Carters' or one that is more approachable, it's important that you recognize and integrate these five essentials:

1. Loving your neighbor starts with the love of God.
2. Reinhabit your neighborhood missionally and emotionally.
3. Redeem the kairos.
4. Have an exponential perspective.
5. Recognize that you are authorized and commissioned by the Lord.

1. It Starts with the Love of God.

The love of God is the most powerful and influential force we have for loving our neighbors. It marks us as being uniquely Christian. This kind of love does not come from us, but from God. We are mere conduits of His love. As Galatians 5:22 points out, love is the fruit of the Spirit. We cannot *try* to love more; we need to *allow* God to love more through us. This may sound like semantics, but there is a marked difference. For those of us who walk by faith as Christians, there is a free flow of God's love ready to course through us, regardless of where we are in our journey. We have the freedom to turn off that free flow through acts of our sinful nature (see Ephesians 5:17). I have grieved and quenched the Spirit many times, but as we grow in our relationship with God, the fruit of the

Spirit, or the character of God, becomes more established in our lives. No one has exhibited this to me more than the late Dallas Willard. I have heard people talk about how he was loved and respected by his students at USC, who came from every walk of life. These were his neighbors.

How did he live this kind of life with them and how can we love our neighbor as ourself? Dallas explained at a Neighborhood Initiative conference how God does this.

"All we have to do is simply follow Jesus' words," Dallas told us. "Of course, loving God with all our heart, soul, mind, and strength comes first. Without that, you can't love your neighbor as yourself. You have to have the resources, the insight to do that, and that comes from our love of God and our devotion of every aspect of our being to His work which He's doing in our world.

"God is present in our cities," he said. "He is there as the great God who created the world and our cities and everything in them. And now He's inducting us and bringing us into His work as we learn in His presence to love our neighbor as ourself.

"When He says the Great Commandment is to love God with all your heart, soul, mind, and strength and your neighbor as yourself, that's one of His great statements about how this is *all* you have to do," Willard said. "If you just do this, everything else will take care of itself. One of the things that we often miss is that His mission in the world is incarnational. It comes through people. Incarnation is not just a theological doctrine. It's a doctrine about how we live. And if we're going to bring Christ to our world, our cities, and our neighbors, then we do it in our own person: skin on skin contact, face to face relationships with others in which we manifest a love that is beyond human possibility and yet is within human actuality because God makes it so."[10]

I want to emphasize that to love your neighbor, you must first receive the love of God and truly love yourself. This is a point that doesn't get addressed enough, and we have many people within the

church who are quick to leave the ways of the Lord for outside plea-
sures. Without knowing the love of God personally, there is a real
danger of serving from a place of the old nature, the place where the
Spirit cannot thrive. As we allow the Lord to love us and change our
hearts, we demonstrate true discipleship to those around us. This
kind of authentic relationship with God is what our culture craves
and needs.

The prerequisite for what we do in our neighborhoods is the
love of God, His love flowing through us, and our love for Him.

2. Reinhabit Your Neighborhood.

Generally, the perspective Christians have when they move into a
new home or apartment is quite different from the perspective missionaries have when they move to their new country of ministry.

When we look for a place to live, we generally look for a place
that best suits us. We ask ourselves questions like:

- Do I like the looks of this place?
- Does it have all the amenities I/we would like for a home?
- Will this place accommodate my/our needs?
- Is this a good price to buy or rent?
- Is this a nice and safe neighborhood?
- Will I like my neighbors?
- If I sell this place, will I get a good price for it?

While these are all legitimate questions when searching for a
place to live, if we want to make a difference in our neighborhood
we need to consider asking the questions that a missionary would
ask as well. Regardless of where you live, it is guaranteed that there
will be people there in need of the love of God.

- Why does the Lord want me to live in this place?
- What is the Lord doing in this neighborhood?

- How does He want me to join Him?
- How can I best serve my neighbors?
- What are the needs of the people who live around me?
- What are my neighbors going through emotionally and how can I be of help?

Because most of us moved into our homes without a ministry mind-set, we need to reinhabit them as missionaries do. Your home will not only be the place you decorate, landscape, and care for your family, but it will become a center for carrying out the Lord's work in your neighborhood. You will begin to see your neighbors as Jesus would, "harassed and helpless, like sheep without a shepherd" (Matthew 9:36). You will have His compassion to care for their needs, whatever they might be.

This is not a command to fix or attend to their every need, but this reinhabitation will strategically place you in reach of loving those in your midst.

3. Redeem the Kairos.

The Greek has two words for time: *chronos* and *kairos*. A kairos moment is one in which time stands still and you are able to be fully present in a situation. If you want to inhabit your neighborhood missionally and emotionally, then "redeeming the kairos" is critical to what the Lord now has for you. This concept may radically change the way you live. This is how Jesus operated, and we see it replicated in the apostle Paul's life.

Paul says in Ephesians 5:15-16, "See then that ye walk circumspectly, not as fools, but as wise, redeeming the *time*, because the days are evil" (KJV, emphasis added). One might assume Paul is saying we must fill every moment of our day with holy and productive activity because the days are evil. However, this is not what Paul is emphasizing. Paul is using the word *kairos* instead of *chronos*, or linear time.

Chronos concerns time as in the 24-hour day. We define our workweeks by the number of hours that we work. We have a list of things to do and only so much time to get everything done. Having a chronos mind-set can make us miss what Paul is saying in Ephesians 5. Paul instructs us to redeem the kairos—to pay attention and take advantage of the opportune times and seasons. Kairos is best referred to as an opportunity. In fact, the New International Version uses "opportunity" instead of "time" in Ephesians 5:16. As parents, we only have a certain season of time to raise our children and then the opportunity is over. Opportunity may refer to a lengthy period of chronos or the short kairos moments that we are to redeem.

The story in chapter 5 of our neighbor Marcy coming to our door to let my wife know that Marcy's car had been broken into is a perfect example of a kairos moment. This was not a lengthy period of time. We could either redeem that moment or miss the unique opportunity before us. I could have given her the money a week later, but the impact of the gift would have meant little if her husband had returned. We have all had one of those experiences when we regret that we missed an opportunity. This is what Paul is emphasizing here: Redeem it. Buy it up for a profitable purpose and invest your whole self in that moment.

In Colossians 4:5 Paul restates redeeming the kairos, and in this account he puts it in the context of those who are outside the church. He says, "Be wise in the way you act toward outsiders; make the most of every opportunity." If you study the life and ministry of Jesus in the Gospels, you will see that this is how He lived. He never seemed to be in a hurry, but invested in every opportunity that came His way.

Many of these opportunities are stories we heard about as children, like the story of Zacchaeus, which is so much more than a children's story. It is the account of a kairos moment. In this moment time almost stood still as Jesus said to him, "Zacchaeus, come down immediately. I must stay at your house today" (Luke

19:5). Jesus capitalized on the opportunity and went to Zacchaeus's house that day. Jesus didn't just call him out of a random crowd. Zacchaeus was already seeking. The moment they crossed paths, Jesus seized the divine moment. He redeemed the kairos.

When it comes to ministering in our neighborhood as Jesus would, we must redeem every opportunity that presents itself to us. We must have eyes as Jesus did to see what our Father is doing and then take advantage of it.

An expert in the law approached Jesus and asked Him what he should do to inherit eternal life. Jesus told him he must love the Lord, and and he must love his neighbor as himself. Wishing to justify himself he asked Jesus, "And who is my neighbor?" (Luke 10:29). In reply Jesus told him the famous story of the Good Samaritan. He pointed out that both religious men, the priest and the Levite, avoided the opportunity to care for the man who had been robbed and left by the side of the road, whereas the Samaritan capitalized on the kairos moment: "When he saw him, he took pity on him. He went to him and bandaged his wounds, pouring on oil and wine. Then he put the man on his own donkey, brought him to an inn and took care of him" (verses 33-34).

When we take advantage of these unique moments, like the Good Samaritan did in the parable, we have the opportunity to live our lives as Jesus did. We can become more like Jesus, as you'll see in Nadine's story.

Nadine's Kairos

"It was two a.m. I know because I glanced at the clock thinking my mom had forgotten her key and was ringing the doorbell to wake me. But when the continuous doorbell and loud raps were followed by a woman's cries, it was apparent that something was wrong. I peered through the shutter at the front door and saw a young woman looking around yelling, 'Please help me, somebody, please!' I thought it was a neighbor, but when she turned and I saw her bloody face I knew this was a stranger.

"As I unlocked the door, I thought, *I don't know what I'm letting into my house. She could be an enemy and my four children are sleeping.* But I decided she needed help and quickly let her in, checking for any danger behind her and locking her in with us. She was drenched in blood, even her teeth, like something out of the violent movies I love so much. She was yelling, 'I'm bleeding. I don't want to die! I don't want to die!' I told her she was safe and that I was going to call 911.

"I told her to sit and she plopped into a chair. While I called for police and an ambulance, my mom came in with paper towels and applied pressure to the dark blood coming from her neck. About six police officers arrived while I was still trying to gather information for the emergency operator about her attacker. It was clear that she wasn't going to say who did this or answer much about what had happened. As the officers assessed the damage, I was shocked at how extensive her stab wounds were: two on the neck, one of them severe, another deep one on her back, and several other smaller ones on her torso. I was surprised that I hadn't felt more compassion. There wasn't much more I could do but gather fresh towels for the police as they tended to her. I did ask God if I shouldn't be doing something, as if this was the perfect opportunity for Him to use me in some grand act of healing, but heard no prompting from Him. However, I did find myself telling her 'Look how brave you are. You are going to be just fine' a couple of times like I was her mom. I later wondered if anyone had ever told her that.

"Oddly enough, my boys slept soundly in the same room, with only a partition between them and the woman. They only awoke after she had been transported some forty-five minutes later. One of my daughters slept through practically the whole ordeal and the other heard everything and decided this was a once-in-a-lifetime scenario she should try and see. The moment she peeked out her window they had already completely covered the young woman in blankets, leaving no real visual of the crime for my daughter to hold in her mind.

"Over the next several hours other officers, detectives, and forensic experts came through. One officer told me she wouldn't have done what I did, but would have left the door closed and called for the police. Several others, however, said I was a Good Samaritan and had saved this girl's life. I learned this twenty-year-old was a mom and a gang member, and I wondered if her life would be impacted by this or remain the same.

"After cleaning up all the blood in the room and in front of the house, I sat in a bath to process what had happened and felt the wave of fear at what *could* have happened. I started asking myself, *What were you thinking?* And I felt God say, 'You know that moment when you thought it was your neighbor? That was me. I was giving you the okay in your subconscious. I was there with you. There wasn't time for more.'"

Nadine saved this young woman's life by opening her door to her and staunching the flow of blood until help arrived. If she had left her on the front porch, she more than likely would have died. We may all have our opinions about what was right or wrong to do in this situation, but the Lord directed Nadine to take care of her. Nadine was in the midst of doing what the Father was doing. She redeemed this extraordinary moment.

When we embrace a kairos approach to life, rather than being driven by the clock or our activities, we can take advantage of opportune moments, as Jesus did, and experience the Lord working through us to accomplish His purpose in the life of another.

4. Have an Exponential Perspective.

Setting expectations too high when you begin ministering in your neighborhood may lead to frustration and defeat. There is a danger of missing the subtle evidence that the Lord is at work if expectations are too lofty. Keep in mind that developing a neighborhood ministry is a process; little by little God's kingdom grows and penetrates the world.

The parable of the mustard seed helps us understand this process: "The kingdom of heaven is like a mustard seed, which a man took and planted in his field. Though it is the smallest of all seeds, yet when it grows, it is the largest of garden plants and becomes a tree, so that the birds come and perch in its branches" (Matthew 13:31-32). In time the mustard seed will take over the whole garden. In the same way, ministry in your neighborhood starts with small acts of kindness and service that grow into what God has in mind. Like the mustard seed, it only takes small expressions of love for God's kingdom to begin to break into your neighborhood.

5. Recognize Your Commission.

You are entering into a work in your neighborhood that is not just a good idea, but something the Lord Jesus Christ has authorized and commissioned you to do. He says in Matthew 28:18-20,

> All authority in heaven and on earth has been given to me. Therefore go and make disciples of all nations, baptizing them in the name of the Father and of the Son and of the Holy Spirit, and teaching them to obey everything I have commanded you. And surely I am with you always, to the very end of the age.

In Jesus exists all power and authority. Jesus, much like a sheriff, deputized His disciples so they would now assume His responsibility, acting on His authority. What responsibility was He passing on to them? They were to extend the invitation into apprenticeship with Jesus, teaching others to do everything they too had been commanded and had witnessed from Him. This invitation wasn't for a select few in the church, but for all who were His disciples. Even as He was returning to heaven, Jesus said to them, "And surely I am with you always, to the very end of the age" (verse 20). His

Spirit would join them, and us, in this work of making disciples. We are all to carry on Jesus' work. When you are involved in making disciples, His presence manifests His favor and the words to speak at the moment.

The Great Commission really has only one command, "make disciples." The word *go* is employed as a participle. *Go* can be translated as "in your going" or "as you go." Jesus was not emphasizing so much to "go" to a certain place, but was pointing out that "as they go," they were to make disciples. With this understanding, disciple-making would take place in the natural flow of one's life. Where does the natural flow of life take us? The places you and I go every day. This is our mission field.

The natural flow of our life will fit into these three categories:

- Common Community: the neighborhood in which you live
- Common Family: your immediate and extended family
- Common Interest: your workplace, school, or any other activity that naturally connects you with people

This is what Jesus was referring to in the Great Commission when He said, As you go "make disciples" (verse 19).

All three categories are important, but when we start by loving those in our own neighborhood (Common Community), which really includes those in our own household, we will more than likely begin to see this love spill into every context of our daily lives. With this love flowing through us, people can't help but be attracted to it and curious about us. Thus, a door is opened for us, and a door is opened for others to see the kingdom.

Chapter 17

The Overall Plan

Before we look at the overall plan for reaching out in our neighborhoods, I would like to point out something that may be helpful for you and your church.

Years ago, in one of our initial meetings about adopting neighborhoods, LAPD Chaplain Ken Crawford said something that has stayed with me to this day. He said every city and neighborhood is different. What works in one neighborhood or community may not work at all in another. You can't create a one-size-fits-all plan. He encouraged us to keep our plan flexible enough so others can adapt it to fit their own neighborhoods.

What follows is an outline of the plan that we have used with our church and that other churches have used as well. You can use the following ideas or go to http://neighborhoodinitiative.com/resources/pastorspackage/ and download various documents to tailor a plan that suits your neighborhood and church.

This first section covers the overall plan for neighborhood ministry, and the second section lists some simple steps to get you started. At the end, you will find ideas for ministering in your neighborhood. These ideas can be adapted for an apartment complex or another setting.

Getting Started

Be Intentional.

Establishing ministry in your neighborhood is more than a good idea or something you are involved with occasionally; it is a commitment to "Love your neighbor as yourself" (Matthew 22:39). There is a marked difference between being nice and doing things for your neighbors when you have the time, and having a deep concern for their welfare and acting on it. Consider how you have taken care of yourself over the years and now love your neighbor in the same manner. If you are intentional it will make a profound change in your neighborhood.

Connect to the Local Church.

Involvement in ministry is always more effective when you come under leadership. It is in this context that God gives favor, direction, protection, and blessing to what He wants to do through you. Let the leadership of your church know of your intention to start a ministry in your neighborhood. You can come under a covering by meeting with one of the leaders on an ongoing basis or by participating in a small group where prayer support is available to you. By connecting with leadership you may also learn about others from your congregation who are willing to help you and even those from other congregations who may live near you who might want to partner with you in your neighborhood.

Establish a Core Group of Intercessors and Other Support People.

You are embarking on frontline ministry, and the Enemy will use everything in his arsenal to impede kingdom movement in your neighborhood. It is essential that you have intercessors to cover and intercede for you as you move out. Don't do it alone. Ask others to come alongside you to pray and help when needed. As the Scriptures teach, "Two are better than one, because they have a good return for their labor" (Ecclesiastes 4:9).

Establish Your Home as a "House of Light" in Your Neighborhood.

Commit your home to the Lord's work and to be a lighthouse in the community. You might want to ask respected leaders to pray over your home and neighborhood. Jesus seems to indicate that the home would become the center for ministry in the world. We keep saying this because it bears repeating: "Whatever town or village you enter, search there for some worthy person and stay at their house until you leave. As you enter the home, give it your greeting. If the home is deserving, let your peace rest on it; if it is not, let your peace return to you. If anyone will not welcome you or listen to your words, leave that home or town and shake the dust off your feet" (Matthew 10:11-14). Throughout the Gospels, the book of Acts, and early church history, we see the home as a strategic place for the spread of the gospel. We're not advocating the abandonment of the established churches, which have their own form of community. We're simply spreading it out to the neighborhood.

Free Up Your Schedule.

Begin to free up your calendar. Make a list of the things you do, and begin to say no to those things that fragment your life and leave you feeling hurried and stressed. These are the same things that will take you away from relationships with your family and your neighbors.

Establish Geographic Boundaries.

Geographic boundaries can be looked at in two ways. The first boundary that you will want to establish is your immediate neighborhood boundary where you will concentrate your ministry. Generally, this will be within walking distance of your home. The second boundary pertains to where you shop and send your children to school (approximately a one-mile radius). Seek to do as much within this area as possible to build relationships with those in your community.

Take Prayer Walks in Your Neighborhood.

As you begin to pray, the Lord will burden your heart for your neighbors and speak to you about them. Meaningful ministry must be grounded in prayer. As you pray and walk, the Lord may open doors for you to talk with your neighbors; take advantage of these special opportunities to get to know them and build relationship.

Observe What God Is Doing.

When it came to ministry Jesus said, "Very truly I tell you, the Son can do nothing by himself; he can do only what he sees his Father doing, because whatever the Father does the Son also does" (John 5:19). As you take time to observe the activities around you, ask for the Father's perspective to understand where He is moving and how you can join Him. For example, look for needs that exist in your neighborhood. While engaged in conversations with your neighbors, be sensitive to the Lord. Be ready to be stirred to respond in some way. You may hear of things that will tip you off to what He is doing. You don't have to be the hands and feet that meet every need, but just those the Spirit is prompting.

Building Relationships

Spend More Time in Your Front Yard.

Become more visible in your neighborhood. For example, make it a practice of playing and/or gardening in your front yard. You might even put some lawn chairs out in the front yard and relax. You will be surprised how people will warm up to you. We live in a very isolated society. Often neighbors do not know each other, so the more time that you spend in your front yard the more you will see them driving or walking by. Smile and wave at those who pass by, even if you don't know them. Take time to talk to walkers and begin to build relationship in natural ways. Take an interest in people and ask them questions. You will find that most people enjoy talking about themselves.

Become a Good Neighbor.
- Be friendly to your neighbors.
- Take care of your property.
- Spontaneously stop by to see your neighbors.
- Look for opportunities to serve them.
- If your dog barks all the time, come up with a solution.
- Borrow something from your neighbor; it gives you a great excuse to see him or her. Don't forget to give it back.
- Here's a great plan: "Do to others as you would have them do to you" (Luke 6:31).
- Look out for each other's property when the other is out of town.

Get to know Your Neighbors.
- Identify the names of your neighbors and other important information about them (for example, children's names, place of employment, birthdays, and so on).
- Volunteer for organizations like the American Heart Association and go door to door asking neighbors if they would like to give to this worthy cause. These organizations will provide you with the names of people on your block.
- Become aware of your neighbors' needs (for example, house, health, food, driving, and so on) for prayer purposes and to see if your Neighborhood Initiative support team can help.
- You might want to put together a map of your neighborhood with the above information on it to help you remember. Engage your neighbors respectfully, being careful not to stalk them. Some may be uneasy if you have information about them that they didn't volunteer.

Spend Time with a Few Neighbors.

Begin spending time with one to two families you have sought out within your neighborhood. Remember the little-by-little principle mentioned on pages 88-89. Share dinner or dessert together where every family contributes to the meal, thereby making everyone feel a part of the experience. If one person or family supplies all the food, it removes the shared experience. As neighbors take part it spills over into other ways of sharing.

Connect with Other Neighborhood Groups.

- Attend your local Neighborhood Watch and/or council meetings. Those who are a part of these meetings generally have a high value for the neighborhood and are good contacts for connecting you with your neighbors. They will also provide you with a better understanding of your neighborhood.
- If time and energy permit, offer to be your Neighborhood Watch representative.

Attend Neighbors' Events.

Christians have a tendency to not attend neighborhood events when neighbors invite them for one reason or another. We feel we are like fish out of water. And yet Jesus was accused of being "a glutton and a drunkard, a friend of tax collectors and sinners" (Matthew 11:19). May we hope to be accused of the same! So, if you are invited to a baby shower, a barbeque or a pool party, a wedding, a funeral, or you name it, attend. This communicates volumes to neighbors.

Find a Purpose to Bring All the Neighbors Together.

- Block party
- Free car wash
- Women's tea
- Movie night

- Volleyball or basketball night
- Neighborhood Watch meeting
- Neighborhood Improvement meeting

Developing Ministry

Identify a Ministry Core.

Begin to pray with your intercessors about a core group of believers for your neighborhood. Locate other believers in your neighborhood, and ask if they would like to help with a neighborhood ministry.

Agree on a Common Purpose.

Bring the matter to God in prayer and identify what the Father is doing in your neighborhood. Each neighborhood is different and the way the Lord works in one neighborhood will be much different than in another. However, you will need to have a vision to be intentional and to have a method to participate in the transformation of your neighborhood. You might not see the details of how this vision will unfold, but it will keep you connected to your purpose and heart for your neighborhood.

Meet the Needs of People in Your Neighborhood.

Often the needs of people will help reveal the Father's plan in your neighborhood. Jesus' ministry abounded with meeting the needs of people. As a word of caution, there were times when Jesus let outstanding needs go unmet. One person cannot do everything. With this in mind, use Jesus' example of returning to the Father often for direction, and don't be afraid to employ others from the neighborhood to help meet the needs that exist. If the task is daunting, ask for your Neighborhood Initiative team to help.

Develop Community Service Teams.

Find other people in your neighborhood who would like to help build community through acts of service and caring. Working together on community service projects deepens relationships and takes the burden off the city's workforce (for example, working with a community organization, helping with a youth program, cleaning up or painting a local school, mentoring, filling in potholes, and so on).

Start a Small Group for Your Neighborhood.
Initially, the small group could be started to accommodate a service project. You might come together for a regular potluck or barbeque, or to cover some reading material like *Laugh Your Way to a Better Marriage* with Mark Gungor or *Financial Peace University* with Dave Ramsey. The group might segue into a Bible study. Give it time to grow into what the Lord has in mind for it.

As those in your neighborhood begin to have more of an interest in spiritual things, you might want to establish a small group for study and prayer as well. The make-up of the group might consist of those in your neighborhood and those from your church. Our desire is that these groups will consist of what we find in Acts 2:

> They devoted themselves to the apostles' teaching and to fellowship, to the breaking of bread and to prayer. Everyone was filled with awe at the many wonders and signs performed by the apostles. All the believers were together and had everything in common. They sold property and possessions to give to anyone who had need. Every day they continued to meet together in the temple courts. They broke bread in their homes and ate together with glad and sincere hearts, praising God and enjoying the favor of all the people. And the Lord added to their number daily those who were being saved. (verses 42-47)

Making Disciples
Ministry in your neighborhood accomplishes more than building friendships and doing things for others; it leads to making disciples. Jesus directed His disciples,

Go and make disciples of all nations, baptizing them in the name
of the Father and of the Son and of the Holy Spirit, and teaching
them to obey everything I have commanded you. And surely I am
with you always, to the very end of the age. (Matthew 28:19-20)

Find a Person of Peace.

Making disciples starts with Jesus' strategy in a neighborhood, finding
a "person of peace." As Jesus directed, look for people in your neighborhood who welcome you. These are neighbors who seem to like
you and who seem to have a unique affinity for one another. Jesus
says, "Whoever listens to you listens to me; whoever rejects you rejects
me; but whoever rejects me rejects him who sent me" (Luke 10:16).

If they like you and listen to you, then you have found people
of peace and you are on your way to making disciples. These are the
ones you are searching for in your neighborhood. They are the key
to your neighborhood and the ones whom God will use to unlock
the ministry of discipleship in your neighborhood. As Jesus said,
"Stay in that house" (verse 7, NASB). Once you have found a person
of peace devote time to the relationship. You might be thinking,
There are more people in my neighborhood I need to contact. You will
have time for that, but your priority is to those who are people of
peace. Remember Jesus' encounter with the woman at the well?
Jesus first took the time to make sure that she understood who He
was. He patiently and graciously revealed who He was and then she
went back and told everyone she knew what He had said. She eventually became the link to winning those in the city of Sychar.

I look at it like spot bowling; if you hit the right spot you hit all
the pins. In the same way, finding the right person in your neighborhood may lead to making many disciples on your block.

Establish a One-on-One Relationship.

When the Lord opens a door for the gospel, show your neighbor the
plan of salvation laid out in the New Testament. There are a number

100 ■ Neighborhood Initiative

of ways to go about this, and there are tools available to help your neighbor understand how he or she can become a child of God. Most importantly, you want to be led by the Holy Spirit as He makes Jesus known through you. The advantage of leading your neighbor into a relationship with the Lord is that you have the unique opportunity to follow up with someone who lives down the street from you. It would be ideal to read together and discuss the book of John or Mark to show him or her what it is to be a follower of Christ. There are also many books and DVD resources available that you will find quite helpful. I highly recommend the Alpha course as an effective teaching tool for unbelievers and new believers alike. Alpha gives everyone the opportunity to explore the meaning of life in a relaxed, friendly setting. The Alpha course usually meets once a week for 10 weeks, including a one-day or weekend getaway. Sessions begin with a meal, followed by a short talk and time to discuss what's been taught (http://alphausa.org/Group/Group.aspx?ID=1000047505).

Start a Small Group.
This kind of group may start in your home or in a neighbor's home. Some of your neighbors may express a desire to meet together to learn about the Bible or becoming a Christian, or even to discuss such subjects as marriage or parenting. (See "Establish a One-on-One Relationship" above for suggestions.)

Join a Community Group.
This is a home group located reasonably close to your neighborhood. A community group is made up of believers and unbelievers who want to know what it is to be followers of Jesus Christ. If your neighbor desires a better understanding of what it means to be a disciple of Jesus, this is an ideal group setting. When you invite your neighbor, assist in the transition as he or she joins in and be sensitive because the context could be threatening.

Attend a Local Church/House Church.
You might invite your neighbor to your church and he or she might feel very much at home with your fellowship. Participation in your local church is good because you can help him or her connect with the people. However, for one reason or another you might find that directing your neighbor to another congregation is a better choice. Churches and people are all very different and what your neighbor is looking for may be different than your needs. For example, you might travel some distance to church but your neighbor prefers to attend one down the street. Be sensitive to the Holy Spirit's leading in this matter.

A Recap: Simple Steps to Start a Neighborhood Ministry

- Seek the Lord's direction. Is it what the Father is doing?
- If you are married, is your spouse wholeheartedly on board with you to minister in your neighborhood?
- If the answers to the above questions are yes, then inform the leadership of your church your intent to begin a ministry in your neighborhood. If your spouse is not interested in partnering with you, you can still develop your own relationships with neighbors, but be careful to listen to God's leading. This might not be the time for further investment in this type of ministry.
- Ask two or three intercessors to support you in prayer as you minister in your neighborhood.
- Pray that the Lord will show you the geographic boundaries for your neighborhood ministry.
- Get to know your neighbors, both adults and children, by name, and begin addressing everyone by name.
- Take prayer walks in your neighborhood and/or pray over a street map.
- Spend time in your front yard.

- Spontaneously stop by your neighbor's home to say hello or to ask to borrow something. Remember to return any borrowed items in a timely manner.
- As the Lord leads you, focus on two or three neighbors that you would like to get to know and invite them over for dinner or dessert.
- Identify other believers in your neighborhood.
- Look for neighborhood needs and try to meet them if possible.
- Think of fun activities to do with your neighbors such as having a block party.

Chapter 18

Resources

Neighborhood Ministry Resources by Category

For and/or by Kids

- "Sunday Sundae": Neighbors gather for sundaes on Sunday.
- Art class for kids.
- Bible study.
- Birthday party organizing.
- Convert your garage into a movie theater for the neighborhood.
- Cooking class for kids.
- Create a library of books for kids.
- Fathers' fishing trip.
- For kids: Leave May Day flower baskets, ring bell, and run away.
- Help with a baby shower.
- Hiking.
- Lend or give books to neighbors to read.
- Outdoor movie night: Project a movie onto a garage or outdoor screen.
- Neighborhood co-op: Babysit, care for pets, bring in mail or newspaper when neighbor is shut-in or on vacation, and so on.
- Neighborhood newspaper or e-mail: Ask neighbors for submissions about the goings on in the community or

your block and write them up periodically. (Children can get involved in this.)
- Put on a neighborhood play.
- Scavenger hunt (great fun for families).
- Start a book club.
- Start a library checkout.
- Story reading for children in the neighborhood.
- Swim/BBQ.
- Take walks or bike rides with neighbors.
- Hold a neighborhood Vacation Bible School at your house, inviting neighbor children. End the week of teaching and games with a carnival hosted by your church.

For and/or by Women
- Bible study.
- Make a local coffee shop your regular hangout alone or with friends. You will support the local business and have time for relationship. You may develop relationships with the staff as well.
- Regular outings to local cultural events or to hear local music.
- Christmas or other holiday shopping or outings.
- Craft or fitness classes.
- Tea party.

For and/or by Men
- Bible study.
- Neighborhood cleanup.
- Sporting event.
- Jogging or biking together.
- Helping other neighbors with maintenance, plumbing, painting, and yard work.
- Helping the elderly, someone with a disability, or anyone in need in the neighborhood.

- Neighborhood basketball or volleyball game.
- Boot camp for exercise.
- Watching the Super Bowl and other sporting events together.
- Going out for breakfast together.

Seasonal

- Fourth of July parade: Decorate bikes, wagons, and pets for a parade.
- Christmas caroling.
- Christmas: Put up lights for neighbors. Include the neighbors in helping other neighbors.
- Clean gutters.
- Halloween: Set up an outdoor picture-taking event for kids in costumes. Use digital or Polaroid camera so children have their photos right away. Offer cider or coffee for the adults.
- Leaf raking.
- Snow removal from driveways and sidewalks.
- Tree trimming.

Maintenance and Repairs

- Ask your neighbors for help when needed.
- Free car wash for the neighborhood. (You might want to add free BBQ hotdogs and drinks while your neighbors wait.)
- Help with home repairs.
- Help with unkempt lawns in the neighborhood.
- Help an older couple with yard work, home repair, and so on.
- Neighborhood windshield washing.
- Outdoor window washing.
- Return empty garbage cans from street.
- Help out a single parent.

Neighborhood Opportunities for Learning Together
- Art class for kids.
- Basic auto repair.
- Bible study.
- Cooking lessons: Barbeque or baking.
- Create a library of books for kids.
- Group gardening classes; celebrate with a big salad.
- Marriage classes.
- Photography lesson during a neighborhood walk.
- Scrapbooking or other craft class.
- Start a book club.
- Story reading for children in the neighborhood.

Fun Ideas Neighbors Can Do Together
- Host a pancake breakfast, in the front yard if possible to let neighbors see what is going on.
- Neighborhood potluck.
- Picture night: Bring favorite pictures; guess who is in the pictures, and so on.
- Progressive dinner or dessert.
- Soup and homemade bread night. (Ask neighbors to bring their own.)
- Watch a major sporting event together.
- Regularly invite a single person to a meal.
- Include neighbors in your private gatherings.

Neighborhood Projects and Ministry Ideas
- As you take a morning walk, put newspapers on neighbors' porches.
- Organize monthly neighborhood parties.
- Organize a "Keep the Neighborhood Beautiful" walk to pick up trash.

Chapter 19

"Will You Be My Neighbor?"

As I was wrapping up this book, I tried to think of a neighborhood story that would be a fitting conclusion. I tossed around different possibilities, but none of them seemed to work. I put my thoughts on hold until I received a call from Mary Alice Pollok, whose elderly neighbor, Jacob, had a hard time recovering after his wife's death. I mentioned Jacob earlier in chapter 5. Here's the rest of that story.

Mary Alice was deep in conversation with her fourteen-year-old son one night. Because she treasures and protects this time with her son, especially as he grows into a young man, she was screening her calls. That night her caller ID revealed it was her eighty-year-old neighbor Jacob.

"Jacob has been calling our home regularly since his wife died about two years ago," Mary Alice said. "He's never seemed to get back on his feet. He had regular bouts of depression, anxiety, and fear—something regular phone calls, evening visits with home-made dinners four to five times a week, and weekend walks didn't seem to relieve. In Jacob's own words, he was 'a crotchety old Jewish man who doesn't make friends easily.'

"What a sight we had become in our community when we would take our walks," Mary Alice said. "A mother of two eighth graders happily chatting with a grumpy, disheveled old man. No one could figure that one out. But God had plans for this friendship."

When Mary Alice answered the phone to see what Jacob needed, she could hear breathing but her neighbor didn't respond to her questions. She threw on her warm coat, told her son not to worry, and "bounded down three flights of stairs and over to the next building where Jacob lived.

"As I approached his home, I could see the front door ajar," Mary Alice said. "I walked in and I saw Jacob on the floor at the bottom of the stairs. He was clutching his chest and having difficulty breathing. It took a split second to realize this was *not* one of his anxiety attacks. I called 911 and heard sirens almost immediately from the fire station up the hill. The paramedics arrived and began to do their work. A paramedic asked if he could speak with me. It took a great deal of effort to disentangle my hand from Jacob's as he was clutching it so tightly. His eyes filled with fear as he said, 'Please don't leave me.' I assured him I wouldn't. The paramedic asked me if I could provide medical information on 'my father.' I told him what I knew about Jacob's mental and physical condition and then explained I wasn't Jacob's daughter. 'Then who *are* you?' he asked. I told him I was just a neighbor."

Mary Alice followed the ambulance in her car and could see "the terror on Jacob's face" as medical personnel lifted him onto a hospital gurney. "I asked the ER receptionist if I could see Jacob," she said. "The receptionist asked if I was a relative, but I said I was just a neighbor."

"You're kidding," the receptionist said, but he allowed her to go back in the triage area to see Jacob.

Mary Alice held Jacob's hand as technicians drew blood and placed EKG patches on his chest. The nurse asked her privately how long her father had been in this deteriorated condition. "I told her what I knew and ended the conversation (yet again) with, 'He's not my father,'" Mary Alice said. "I'm just a neighbor."

Shortly after they wheeled Jacob into another room for further testing, the attending physician thanked Mary Alice for keeping Jacob calm and asked the question she already knew was coming. "How are you related to Jacob?"

"I'm not related," Mary Alice said. "I'm just a neighbor."

"I wish I had a neighbor like you," the doctor said.

I think we all would like to have a neighbor like Mary Alice. More importantly, this is what our neighbors need from us, whether or not they realize it. In each case, when those in the hospital asked her if she was a relative and found out that she was just a neighbor, they shook their heads in amazement. Sadly, we live in a day when finding a good neighbor is a rarity. I often think of the State Farm jingle, "Like a good neighbor, State Farm is there."

Good neighbors are few and far between. Wouldn't it be wonderful if the church stepped up to become the good neighbor? As Mary Alice left the emergency room, the doctor asked her with a giggle laced in seriousness, "Will you be my neighbor?"

I think that's the silent appeal of neighborhoods today.

Will we respond?

Notes

1. For more in-depth treatment of this topic, see the chapter "Pastors as Teachers of the Nations," Dallas Willard, *Knowing Christ Today* (NY: HarperCollins, 2009).
2. ALPHA endorsement for June 20, 2009, conference.
3. Dallas Willard, personal conversation with author, 2011.
4. Rick Rusaw and Eric Swanson, *The Externally Focused Church* (Loveland, CO: Group, 2004), 17.
5. Michael Green, *Evangelism in the Early Church* (Grand Rapids, MI: Eerdmans, 1970), 210.
6. Rodney Stark, *The Rise of Christianity* (Princeton, NJ: Princeton University Press, 1996), 7.
7. Jerry Root, "Evangelism as Sacrament," *Christianity Today*, April 2011, vol. 55, no. 4, 67.
8. artofneighboring.com.
9. George Barna, *Grow Your Church from the Outside In*, Barna Group, https://www.barna.org/component/virtuemart/books/grow-your-church-from-the-outside-in-softcover-detail?Itemid=0.
10. Dallas Willard, A *Heart-Felt Word to Pastors and Leaders*, http://www.youtube.com/watch?v=HJeWEFV-bUs&feature=youtube.